SECOND EDITION

creativity NOW

Get inspired, create ideas and make them happen!

JURGEN WOLFF

PEARSON

Harlow, England • London • New York • Boston • San Francisco • Toronto • Sydney
Auckland • Singapore • Hong Kong • Tokyo • Seoul • Taipei • New Delhi
Cape Town • São Paulo • Mexico City • Madrid • Amsterdam • Munich • Paris • Milan

PEARSON EDUCATION LIMITED

Edinburgh Gate
Harlow CM20 2JE
Tel: +44 (0)1279 623623
Fax: +44 (0)1279 431059
Website: www.pearson.com/uk

First published in Great Britain in 2009
Second edition published 2012

ISBN: 978-0-273-77047-3

British Library Cataloguing-in-Publication Data
A catalogue record for this book is available from the British Library

Library of Congress Cataloging-in-Publication Data
Wolff, Jurgen, 1956-
Creativity now : get inspired, create ideas, and make them happen! / Jurgen Wolff. -- 2nd ed.
p. cm.
Includes index.
ISBN 978-0-273-77047-3 (pbk.)
1. Creative thinking. 2. Creative ability. 3. Brainstorming. I. Title.
BF408.W63 2012
153.3'5--dc23
2012007190

10 9 8 7 6 5 4 3 2 1
16 15 14 13 12

Text design by Design Deluxe
Typeset in 9.5pt Univers condensed by 30
Printed and bound in Malaysia (CTP-VVP)

Dedicated to the memory of Linda Ryan and Chris Wicking, whose greatest creation was the love they inspired in their families and friends.

contents

2 originating

3 applying

4 adapting

Creative Success Manifesto

THE PRINCIPLE

The journey to creative success is at least as rewarding as arriving

Before you begin your creative endeavour it may help to stop and think about what creative success means to you: its requirements, its costs, its rewards. This is my creative success manifesto – I invite you to make up your own.

1 Success is what you say it is

If getting to number one on the *New York Times* bestseller list makes you happy, great. If writing a blog that 100 people follow passionately makes you happy, or writing one poem a night that nobody else ever sees, that's what success is for you. It's your brain, your heart, your life – don't let anybody hijack it with their definition of success.

2 Commercial success can take a year or a hundred years

J. K. Rowling got there fast. Van Gogh didn't. Even finding those 100 passionate followers can take time. Don't define the journey only by the outcome.

3 Fewer than 1 per cent of people have to buy what you do

Not everybody wants to profit financially from their creative activity, but if you do, if 1 per cent of the people in the USA – 1 person out of 100 – buys what you offer you'll have more than 3 million sales. In the UK that would be about 600,000. If you happen to live in China, you're really in luck.

4 Start by finding one person who likes what you do

It helps to have a champion, somebody who believes in you. Your belief in yourself generates 1 unit of self-belief. You plus a champion generates 100. (Psychology maths is different.)

5 Crazy is the first step

Every breakthrough is considered a crackpot idea at first. Of course, some are crackpot ideas. You can't tell the difference until you transform the idea into something real.

6 Ready, fire, aim

Most creative people want their work to be seen. However, many never take their ideas out into the world because they want to be sure it's the right time and that they have all the resources they need. It will never be exactly the right time and you may never have all the resources you need. Get a prototype out there, see what happens, adjust and persist.

7 The second best time to start

The best time to start doing your creative work was ten years ago. Look at the clock. What time is it? That's right, the second best time to start.

8 If at first you don't succeed, don't try, try again

At least don't try the same thing again and again. Hit yourself on the head with a hammer (you may imagine this instead of doing it if you prefer). How did it feel? Do you think it will feel any different if you do it again? If you do, go ahead. If at first you don't succeed, try something different. Continue until you find the one that works.

9 Failing feels crappy

Motivational speakers make it sound like failing is noble. Maybe it is, but it sure doesn't feel noble. They claim Edison said something like 'I didn't fail 3,000 times to find a workable light bulb filament, I just eliminated 3,000 ways not to do it so that I could find the one that worked.' I bet around the 2,000th try he threw that bulb to the ground, stomped on it, took a stiff drink and yelled at his wife. Yes, we have to deal with disappointing results and rejection, but we won't like it.

10 The only way to fail

You can fail only if you stop. If on the last day of your life you still aren't on the *New York Times* bestseller list or your blog has only 99 passionate followers, or you never quite got the hang of rhyme scheme, so what? If you believed in what you were doing you probably had a hell of a ride. That's what it's all about.

dreaming

1

Sometimes you feel inspired, sometimes you don't.

Sometimes the ideas flow, sometimes they don't.

Why leave it to chance?

In this part you'll find 25 ways to get yourself into the state of mind that invites new ideas.

for Baroque

THE PRINCIPLE

Music stimulates your creativity

Music may or may not have 'charms that soothe the savage breast', but it does seem to have the power to stimulate the sluggish brain.

Research has shown that Baroque music synchronises brain waves at about 60 cycles per second, and this relaxed alpha state is the frequency associated with creativity. Try Vivaldi's 'The Four Seasons' or Pachelbel's 'Canon in D' or Bach's 'Air in D'.

It's worth doing your own research by listening to different kinds of music to discover the effects it has on you when you're in different moods.

If stress gets in the way of your creativity, you may benefit by using easy-listening music or Gregorian chant. For this purpose, I'm partial to the music of J. J. Cale.

If your energy is low, turning up the speakers and listening to rock music may get your brain cells sparking. Try some classics from Creedence Clearwater Revival.

To get into a problem-solving frame of mind, choose upbeat music. A University of Toronto study revealed that volunteers were better able to solve challenging word puzzles after thinking positive thoughts and listening to upbeat music. It's another excuse to listen to that *Mamma Mia!* soundtrack.

You may even want to create a soundtrack for each of your different creative activities. Russian novelist Boris Akunin told the *Wall Street Journal* that before he begins writing, he plays five or ten minutes of music to get into the right mood. For a tragic mood he favours Mahler, for a tender mood he goes for early Beatles.

There's another way you can add music to your creativity toolbox: wait until you are in a creative mood naturally, then put on a song or album you don't normally play but that supports the mood. Do this on two or three separate occasions, each time using the same music.

Thereafter, when you don't feel creative but would like to, put on that music and it will create the mood by association.

Website bonus

At **www.CreativityNowOnline.com**, click on the 'Creativity Now!' button. Bonus 1 is a guided visualisation with music to energise your creative thinking.

Go away

THE PRINCIPLE

A mini-break clears the way for new ideas

We've all had the experience of getting away from our usual demands and routine and returning feeling refreshed and full of new ideas.

Sadly, it's not possible to take off two weeks for a trip to a tropical island every time we need inspiration.

Fortunately, you can get away from it all without going very far. Here are six ways to do it:

1. **Go to the park.** There's something about being surrounded by greenery and fresh air that immediately helps you switch to a different way of thinking. Even just taking a walk through a park during your lunch break can help.

2. **Try a flotation tank.** In many cities there are facilities where you can float in a tank filled with salt water heated to body temperature, with no or minimal light and sound. After a short period of this sensory deprivation, your mind stops its chatter.

3. **Create a do-it-yourself float.** If you can't find or don't want to pay for a session in a flotation tank, fill your bathtub, put on an eye mask and have a long soak. If there are distracting noises in your environment, use earplugs as well or put on soothing music.

4. **Find an unpopular coffee shop in which to do your work.** They'll be too grateful for your custom to move you on, and you'll have a quiet atmosphere that's different from your usual surroundings. My sometime retreat is a pub with service so rubbish that nobody goes there. Except me.

5. **Go to the library or a church.** Both are havens of quiet where you can get away from excess stimuli. If you're stressed out at an airport, look for the chapel or prayer room – it's probably not a good idea to get out your laptop, but you can sit and think.

6 **Swap homes with a friend for a couple of days.** People do home exchanges when they go on holiday, so why not do the same with friends just for a weekend? Even if they live nearby, the surroundings will be different enough to get you out of your rut.

Remember how to play

THE PRINCIPLE

Playing is the most creative state

Picasso said, 'Every child is an artist. The problem is to remain an artist once we grow up.' That applies to creativity in general.

In his wonderful book *Orbiting the Giant Hairball* (Viking/Allen Lane), artist Gordon Mackenzie relates how he used to go into American schools and ask the children how many of them were artists, too. The 6-year-olds all raised their hands. With third-graders, who were 10, only about a third of them responded that way. When asked the same question at the age of 12, out of a group of 30, only 1 or 2 would raise their hands, hesitantly.

To return to the state of creativity that children have naturally, we have to do what they do – play.

Play can take just about any form. When the great pioneer of psychology, Carl Jung, felt that he had lost direction, he would go into his garden and play with little stones.

The important thing is to do it for its own sake. If you make a drawing, do it just to enjoy the process, not to try to create something others will admire. In fact, it's a good idea to decide beforehand that if your form of play is to make something, you will destroy it when you're done, or at least not show it to anybody.

Has it been so long that you can't think of anything to play? Here are a few ideas to get you started:

- Scribble on a piece of paper, then turn the scribbles into drawings of people or objects (remember, it's not art, it's playing – it doesn't have to be artistically good).

- Play a card game that you enjoyed as a child. Or just make one up. Turn up cards one at a time. If you get four hearts in a row, you get to have a muffin.
- Buy a yo-yo.
- Get some modelling clay and make some figures. If you're angry at somebody, get some pins and do clay voodoo.
- Walk down the street pretending to be your favourite superhero, and imagine yourself solving minor crises. 'Look, Superman/Superwoman, that driver ignored the zebra crossing, use your vision heat rays to melt his tyres!'
- Spend some time with a child – your own or a friend's – and find out what they want to play and join in. Play by their rules!

Website bonus

At www.CreativityNowOnline.com, click on the 'Creativity Now!' button. Bonus 2 is a set of games to get you started playing.

[illegible]y? What? When? [illegible]here? How?

THE PRINCIPLE

The answer is in the questions

If you've ever spent time around a small child, you'll know they love to ask questions. Especially 'why?' (or, more accurately, 'why!!!???').

It can be maddening but it also reflects the curiosity and hunger for learning that tends to dim as we grow up. The way to wake it up again is to ask lots of questions.

As adults, usually we interpret 'why?' as a challenge. If you change your state of mind to consider it simply as a prompt to learn more, it becomes a great way to open your mind to new ideas.

But don't limit yourself to 'why?' – also try lots of 'why not?', 'what?', 'when?', 'where?' and 'how?' questions.

It's not a search for factual answers, it's a way to be open to more possibilities.

For instance, let's say you walk to your favourite coffee shop for a cappuccino. Along the way, here are some questions that might pop into your mind:

- Why do I always walk to the coffee shop this way?
- What's another route I could take that might show me some new sights?
- Why is that woman smiling like that? What might be going on in her life?
- Why don't I buy a bouquet from that flower shop and give it to my significant other? Or to myself? Or to the next person I see?
- Where else can I get a coffee today for a change?
- How many people between here and the coffee shop will be on their mobile phones? What are most of them talking about?

When are you going to start asking more questions? Where will you be when you start? What interesting new thoughts will you have? (I'll stop now. Your turn.)

Create your space

THE PRINCIPLE

Having a dedicated space feeds your creative mood

I hope that, like me, you have a great home office or study, lined with bookshelves with one of those ladders that goes around on a rail, a roaring fireplace, a view of the Thames, and of course a manservant who brings you chocolate when he intuits that your creative energy is flagging.

All right, I lied. I don't have a view of the Thames.

Or a few of the other things. At this stage I am lucky enough to have a nice home office, but at other points I've had to make do with a desk in front of the window of my living room, and, once, a tiny table in a room that flooded whenever it rained.

Some set-ups are better than others, obviously, but here's the important thing: you deserve a space, however small or large, that is yours and yours alone.

If all you can find is a computer table in the kitchen, that's fine, but make it off-limits to the kids and anybody else. Mark your territory with some stuff that you find stimulating (more about this in the next section). If you want a plant but don't have much room, go for a little cactus (which also discourages cats from settling down on your desk).

IKEA and others sell desks that can be closed up easily and take very little room. You can make do with even less by creating a portable office. This might consist of your laptop, some notebooks, an accordion file and some framed pictures that you put on the working surface (like the kitchen table).

However grand or modest it may be, remember: you have a right to your own creative space. Insist on it!

Get the right stuff

THE PRINCIPLE

The images and items around you can stimulate your creativity

Have you outfitted your creative space with pictures, items and colours that encourage creativity?

If not, what would do the job?

Usually we think of zany stuff and I have my share of it in my home office: a Frankenstein head, a large rubber statue of Homer Simpson carrying a doughnut on his back, some figures from *The Nightmare before Christmas*, and a plaster sculpture of Uncle Scrooge diving into a bathtub full of money.

Here are some other ideas:

- plants and flowers
- posters or postcards
- a rear-view mirror attached to your computer
- inspirational quote cards you make yourself
- a symbol of something you hope to achieve.

Colour is important, too. My office is two-tone: red and yellow. You might prefer something more restful.

For visual stimulation, I like to collect the kind of postcards you often find in racks in cafés, bars and gyms. Most of them have some kind of interesting image and every day or so I'll put a new one on my desk. If you prefer, you can buy postcards of great art at a museum shop or book store.

Changing the items is important because even the most inspirational pictures or objects lose their power when you get used to seeing them every day.

One option that adds an element of surprise: set up a trading arrangement with a creative friend, so that every month each of you lends the other half a dozen pictures or other items you find stimulating.

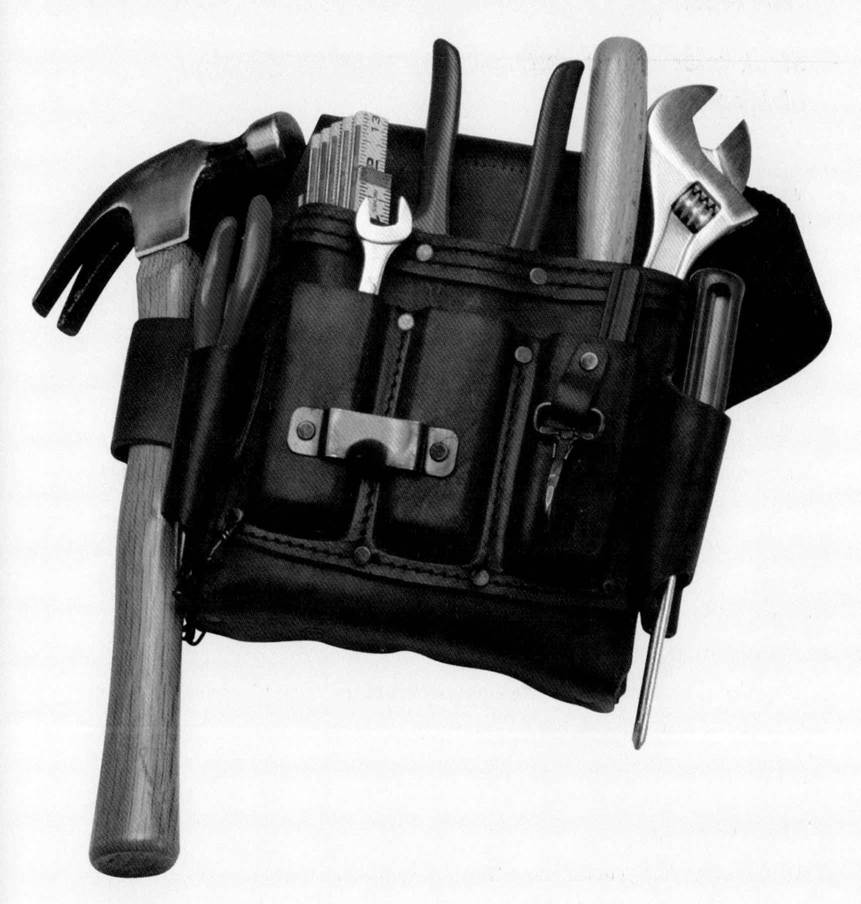

Be a streetcomber

THE PRINCIPLE

Seek interesting stuff and you shall find it. And photograph it

At the Creativity World Forum of 2008, Richard Stomp, an innovation and strategy manager in the Netherlands, suggested that to be creative you should try 'streetcombing' – like beachcombing, but on the streets. Just as a beachcomber roves the beach looking for objects of value or interest, a streetcomber does the same along streets. The streetcomber takes pictures of anything and everything that seems interesting in any way.

Pick a part of town that has a lot of new shops, a lot of foot traffic and a lot of young people. What will catch your attention? It might be a sign, a window display, a mannequin with an interesting expression, a discarded note – anything.

Turn off your inner editor at this stage, otherwise you'll waste time wondering if the thing really is interesting, what you will do with the photo, etc.

The streetcombing process is not about using these images. Although they may give you ideas for settings, characters, or even entire stories, for now you're just trusting the process and gathering images. The very act of looking for interesting stuff to photograph causes a mind shift.

Website bonus

At www.CreativityNowOnline.com, click on the 'Creativity Now!' button. Bonus 3 is a set of photos from one of my own streetcombing expeditions.

Get physical!

THE PRINCIPLE

Movement helps the brain as well as the body

A study cited in the *British Journal of Sports Medicine* reported that exercise enhances both mood and creativity. Another study, reported in the *Creativity Research Journal*, confirmed that the increases in creativity were present both when the test was administered immediately and when it was administered two hours after the activity.

What kind of exercise? In the studies, it was 'moderate aerobic exercise' – in other words, enough to get your heart beating faster, but not so demanding that you're gasping for air. This might include fast walking, jogging or using a cross-trainer or stepper, or even continuous vigorous vacuuming. Some creative people swear by Pilates, others by yoga.

Writer Dan Brown found another way of getting his blood moving: hanging upside-down using a pair of gravity boots. You strap yourself into the boots, then hang like a bat (hooks on the boots go over the bar that you've fixed to a sturdy door frame). The most strenuous part is getting into position, although you can also do some exercises while you're hanging around. Other famous users include Bruce Wayne/Batman in the movie *Batman*, Richard Gere in *American Gigolo* and Uri Geller.

I tried this once, many years ago. The only thing I felt was that my eyeballs were about to pop out and shoot across the room. Maybe if I'd stayed upside-down a little longer I would have written *The Da Vinci Code* and now be very, very rich.

Beneficial effects come from less exotic approaches, of course. Just running in place for a few minutes, using a stationary bike or going up and down the nearest set of stairs will all get your blood flowing faster and more oxygen to your brain.

However you do it, regularly get moving and you'll notice improvements in your creativity as well as your health.

Lose your limited thinking

THE PRINCIPLE

Just because you can't do it doesn't mean it can't be done

Often we stop ourselves from thinking big because we immediately jump to the practicality of the idea. If it's not something we can do ourselves, we tend to dismiss it.

Over time, we train ourselves to think small.

That's the opposite of what we should be doing. At least at the start, we should allow ourselves to have what authors James Collins and Jerry Porras call 'Big Hairy Audacious Goals' – BHAGs for short.

If there are aspects of the project you can't do yourself, these days it's easy to find others to do it (you'll find more details in the 'Outsource' section in Part 3).

Here's a better way to think when you have your next big idea: 'I know this can be done; my challenge will be finding the easiest and best way to do it.'

From now on, keep an ideas notebook, folder or box file. Every time you have an idea, especially a Big Hairy Audacious Goal, jot it down without judgement and put it away. The more ideas you honour by recording them, the more will flow.

Website bonus

At www.CreativityNowOnline.com, click on the 'Creativity Now!' button. Bonus 4 is a couple of pages from my BHAG journal.

You are not under arrest!

THE PRINCIPLE

Overcoming the 'impostor syndrome' unleashes your creativity

Many people suffer from the 'impostor syndrome', the fear that they are incompetent or unworthy and will be found out any day and stripped of their jobs and reputation, if not actually arrested.

For example, successful musician Moby told *The Times* magazine, 'I've never really trusted what success I've had. I feel it to be fraudulent, chimerical and liable to be taken away from me in an instant.'

Talking about her Oscar, actress Jodie Foster told *60 Minutes*: 'I thought everybody would find out, and they'd take the Oscar back. They'd come to my house, knocking on the door, "Excuse me, we meant to give that to someone else. That was going to Meryl Streep."'

I didn't make up the name 'impostor syndrome' – it's a phenomenon that has been studied for years and several books have been written about it. Dr Valerie Young has led workshops for over 30,000 people in how to overcome it. She says 70 per cent of all people reported feeling at one time or another like their success is a fraud (you'll find more information at her website, www.impostersyndrome.com).

Probably this fear stems at least in part from the expectation that some day we'd feel grown up and able to handle everything, just like our parents pretended to be able to do. When this doesn't happen, we think there's something wrong with us.

There is. It's called being human.

When we feel like impostors, it causes anxiety that can block our creativity. If this is an issue for you, the first step to overcoming it is to acknowledge that most of the rest of the world suffers from it too. And if we're all imposters, the odds that *you* will be found out are minimal.

Website bonus

At www.CreativityNowOnline.com, click on the 'Creativity Now!' button. Bonus 5 is a fun gallery of actual impostors.

Make up a story

THE PRINCIPLE

Making up stories warms up your brain

A great way to limber up your mind is to start making connections, and there's nothing the creative mind likes better than making up stories. Randomly pick one element from each of the columns below, so you have TWO CHARACTERS, an EMOTION and a SETTING.

Spend 60 seconds making up a story by mashing them up. If it's good, write it down and send it to George Lucas because this is exactly how he came up with *Star Wars*.* Otherwise, just use it to get your brain warmed up.

First character	Second character	The emotion	The setting
Police officer	Nurse	Jealousy	Pub
Alien	Accountant	Envy	London Eye
Gardener	Doctor	Lust	Slough
Schoolboy	Gangster	Revenge	Hospital

For example, let's say we randomly choose Gardener, Gangster, Revenge and London Eye. Our story might be that a rich gangster's **gardener** overhears his plan to steal a hugely valuable painting from the National Gallery. The gardener blackmails the **gangster** for 10 per cent of the proceeds. With this money, the now former gardener starts living it up. A beautiful woman approaches him and suggests they hire a pod on the **London Eye** so they can have some privacy to do naughty things. He agrees, but when their pod is at the top she throws him out – the first fatality on the London Eye. We realise she's the gangster's girlfriend and has exacted **revenge** ... Crime does not pay! Hey, it doesn't have to be great, it's just an exercise!

Your turn!

* I made that up.

Go fishing with Edison

THE PRINCIPLE

Pretending to be busy gives you time to think

Thomas Edison is one of the great heroes in the annals of creativity, a man tireless in his pursuit of inventions and breakthroughs. He was also an avid fisherman and (naturally) invented a fishing rod.

James Newton, who knew Edison personally, wrote: 'When Mr. Edison ran into a particularly difficult problem, he took his constantly expanding knowledge, a pole, line and hook down to his dock and fished.'

Edison often came back without any fish and only later revealed why. He wrote: 'Because it was my fishing time, my staff did not disturb me, and as I used no bait, the fish did not disturb me either!'

Why bother with the fishing equipment? Why not just sit quietly somewhere and think? Because if anybody sees you just sitting around apparently doing nothing, they will assume you are fair game for a chat or free to solve one of their problems. The idea that you might be thinking never occurs to most people.

Therefore, come up with a cover activity. Sitting with a notebook open before you and a pen in your hand may be enough to do it. Otherwise, ponder a portable chessboard or pretend to be texting on your mobile. Then you'll be left alone to do the real work – in your mind.

Use a mind machine

THE PRINCIPLE

Entraining your brain waves puts you in a creative state

Brain waves operate at different frequencies that are associated with different states of alertness and mental activity.

Beta waves are associated with normal concentration and alertness.

Alpha waves are associated with deep relaxation and creativity.

Theta waves are associated with the half-asleep/half-awake state.

Delta waves are associated with deep sleep.

As the brain waves slow, there is also increased synchronisation between the two hemispheres of the brain. One method for guiding your brain waves to the desired frequency is *entrainment*. Basically, a series of tones and flashing lights match your likely brain waves and then change their rhythm and your brain follows.

The equipment consists of headphones, dark glasses with LEDs on the inside and a control unit. It can be set for different sessions and different periods of time, depending on whether you want to use it for relaxation or stimulation. You lie down or sit in a relaxed position and close your eyes (the LEDs shine through your lids).

Although formal research on the effects is limited, many people have found them useful. On Channel 5's *The Gadget Show*, a model called the Mindspa was chosen by every member of the focus group over two other technologies to reduce stress. I use a basic model called Sirius for dealing with jet lag and stress and for regenerating when I haven't had enough sleep.

However, due to the flashing lights, these machines should not be used by anyone who suffers from epilepsy, brain damage, visual photosensitivity or macular degeneration. If in doubt, always consult your doctor first.

There are a number of UK outlets where you can buy this kind of equipment, including www.meditations-uk.com. The devices range in price from approximately £99 to £275 (the one I use is one of the least expensive). If you don't have the time and patience for traditional meditation, using a mind machine could be a shortcut to increasing relaxation, focus and creativity.

Website bonus

At www.CreativityNowOnline.com, click on the 'Creativity Now!' button. Bonus 6 is a closer look at my mind machine and how I use it.

Find a mentor

THE PRINCIPLE

You can learn to be more creative by modelling your favourite genius

Wouldn't it be great if you could learn from Thomas Edison, Linus Pauling, Steve Jobs, Richard Branson, Stephen Hawking, Abraham Lincoln, Marie Curie, Nikolai Tesla, Vincent van Gogh, or your other favourite genius?

They may be unavailable due to being busy or dead, but just about every genius in any area either wrote or was written about. In many cases, you can find out not only what influenced them but also their thought processes, in books like *How to Think Like Leonardo da Vinci* by Michael Gelb (Element) and *Socrates' Way: Seven Keys to Using Your Mind to the Utmost* by Ronald Gross (published by Jeremy P. Tarcher).

You'll find in many cases that people who were great in one area were not necessarily so admirable in their private lives. But that's OK, you don't need to model your entire life on them, only the parts you want to emulate.

As you read books by and about these people, here are some questions to keep in mind:

- What drove them to be creative?
- What kinds of questions did they ask?
- What kinds of obstacles did they overcome? What did they learn from each one?
- What kept them going when their ideas were ridiculed or resisted?
- What parallels can you find between what they did and what you want to do?

The best teachers are always the people who have done what you wish to do – so why not let the greatest geniuses help you get into the right frame of mind?

Dare to daydream

THE PRINCIPLE

Daydreaming is an essential form of creativity

Probably every worthwhile invention or discovery has appeared in a daydream before it took form in the real world. Yet as children we're taught that daydreaming is a waste of time, a bad habit, a sign of laziness. Yes, there's a time and place for it (it's not so good while driving or operating machinery, for instance), but if you want to turn your brain into a creativity factory, daydreaming is a crucial skill.

Daydreaming is best for imagining the outcome: the way things will be when you've solved a problem, created a work of art or otherwise expressed your creativity.

In these kinds of daydreams there are no obstacles, nobody making fun of your idea, no self-doubts about whether it's possible or practical. With that freedom you can imagine your project or ideas in their purest form.

One of US comedian Steve Wright's lines is, 'I was trying to daydream, but my mind kept wandering.' It's a joke, of course, but there's some truth in it, too. All too often, perhaps remembering some stern teacher, we try to snap ourselves out of such an impractical waste to time.

Don't snap out of it! Stay in it and explore.

Eventually, using methods in Parts 2 and 3 of this book, you can start to figure out which ideas to concentrate on and then how to turn those into reality, but for now your assignment is to let your mind drift where it will.

Record your night dreams

THE PRINCIPLE

Your dreams are a great source of creative ideas

There's a long list of inventors, writers and others who have had breakthrough ideas in their night dreams:

- Mary Shelley's novel *Frankenstein* was inspired by a dream.
- Scientist Friedrich Kekule dreamed the unusual structure of the Benzine molecule.
- Elias Howe dreamed how to change the design of his invention, the sewing machine, so it worked correctly.
- Robert Louis Stevenson dreamed the plot of *Dr Jekyll and Mr Hyde*.
- The tune for 'Yesterday' came to Paul McCartney in a dream.

No wonder Stevenson said that dreams occur in 'that small theatre of the brain which we keep brightly lighted all night long'.

Of course, the vast majority of dreams don't include breakthrough ideas, but even the more routine ones may have some message for you from your subconscious mind. If you don't remember and record them, these messages and inspirations will go to waste.

If you think you don't dream often or you can't remember your dreams, here's an easy process to follow:

1 Put a pad or a journal and a pen by your bedside.

2 Just before your sleep, tell yourself that you will remember your dreams.

3 When you wake up, jot down anything you remember from the dreams you had. At first you may remember only small bits and pieces. Record them anyway, because with practice you'll remember more and more.

4 Do this every night and even when you take a nap.

You may find that some day you'll owe your success to a dream.

Transform your inner critic

THE PRINCIPLE

Your harsh inner critic can be turned into a constructive inner guide

Most people carry a harsh inner critic around with them. It can take one or more forms: a voice in your head, a feeling in the pit of your stomach or elsewhere, or a visual image of some kind.

It tends to pop up when you think big or get excited about doing something new or different. Its message usually is something like these:

> **'What makes you think you can do this?'**
>
> **'This has never been done before – there must be a good reason!'**
>
> **'You'll botch this just like you botch most things.'**
>
> **'Nobody will want this.'**

In other words, it sends you negative messages that are far harsher than any you'd ever send to a friend. Like an overly protective parent, it's trying to save you from disappointment and rejection, but in the process it also 'saves' you from success.

It's time to turn your harsh critic into a constructive guide who knows when to chime in (unlike the critic, who often shows up way too early and nips any new ideas in the bud).

Begin by imagining what your constructive inner guide would sound/feel/look like. Get a strong sense of when and how it would give you feedback. Then, the next time your inner critic pops up, imagine it changing into the inner guide you have imagined. This inner guide may choose to be silent (if it's too early for feedback), or it may have a specific suggestion, or it may just give you encouragement.

Your inner critic may be stubborn at first, but if you transform it each time it shows up, eventually it will yield to the constructive inner guide and you'll find a new freedom of thought coming to you naturally.

Website bonus

At www.CreativityNowOnline.com, click on the 'Creativity Now!' button. Bonus 7 is an audio track giving you more information on the inner critic and how to transform it.

Go back to pen and paper

THE PRINCIPLE

Reconnecting your hand and your brain stimulates creativity

How long has it been since you've written anything by hand? For most people it has been a long time, and for the current generation of youngsters it's becoming almost a lost art. Even the tradition of passing notes in class now happens in the form of texts between mobiles. But it may be that what we gain in ease and speed, we lose in terms of the direct connection between head and hand.

In an article in *New York* magazine, Sam Anderson put it this way: 'Handwriting makes one's relationship to words intensely personal.'

Poet Robert Graves observed, 'A true poet's handwriting corresponds with his inimitable personal rhythm.'

You don't have to be a poet to experience this connection.

Experiment using pen and paper when you're kicking around ideas. Don't feel you have to use any of those formal formats you learned in school, like outlines with roman numerals. Try using mind maps (see 'Use mind maps' in Part 2) or your own way of getting down your thoughts, including doodles, colour pens, coloured paper, even cutting out and pasting pictures from magazines.

By going back to pen and paper, you may find yourself returning to a point in your childhood when it was fun to explore ideas with words and pictures, and when ideas flowed so easily you didn't even notice the process.

Stuff your head with facts

THE PRINCIPLE

To incubate great ideas, your mind needs facts to work with

The standard definition of creativity includes reference to the fact that most new ideas are just new combinations of existing ideas.

You need to have a lot of facts swirling around in your brain before you have the exhilarating experience of coming up with a new one.

The general model is to learn as much as possible and then forget all about it for a while. Quite often the 'Eureka!' breakthrough idea comes in that second phase when you've stopped thinking about the challenge. Obviously some kind of gestation period takes place before the new idea is born.

However, in the first phase it's important to distinguish facts from beliefs or assumptions. Galileo studied the facts about the planets, but he questioned the assumption that the earth was at the centre of the universe and was circled by the sun, moon and stars. He realised that this belief was rooted in religion, not in science.

He is known as the father of *observational* astronomy because he based his conclusions on what he observed rather than what he was told. That makes him a great model for the modern creative person (even if he did have to spend the last years of his life under house arrest on orders of the Roman Inquisition – who said the creative path is easy?).

So while you devour facts about your field, don't also swallow the assumptions that often hide among them. And when you've packed your brain, relax and let your subconscious mind do the work ... and get ready for new ideas to pop up when you least expect them.

Take a nap

THE PRINCIPLE

Short naps leave you refreshed and more creative

The Spanish, Greeks and Italians have known it for a long time: a nap in the afternoon is a good thing.

The North American Space Agency confirmed it with a study that showed a 34 per cent increase in performance following a 26-minute nap. (Do you notice that statistics never seem to come in odd numbers?)

Nap expert Dr Sara C. Mednick (author of *Take a Nap! Change Your Life* – and no, I'm not making that up) says that different lengths of nap have different benefits. To increase alertness, try 20 minutes, for better memory try 40, and for increased creativity, it's 90 minutes.

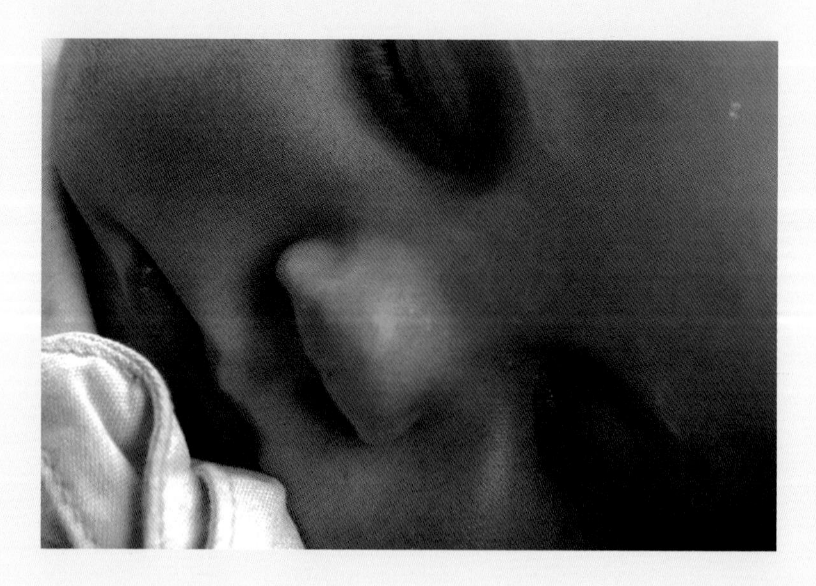

Some businesses have even installed 'energy pods' in which their employees can catch 'forty winks'. Cisco is one of them, and Vinayak Sudame, an engineer there, told the *New York Times* that taking a 10- to 15-minute nap helps him return to work with a 'reorganised perspective'.

The good news is that you already have an energy pod in your home. It's called a bed.

Do your own experiments with different lengths of nap to see what effect they have for you. I find that after a nap of 20–30 minutes, I'm ready to return to my work refreshed and with a clear head; but if I sleep for 30–45 minutes, I tend to wake up groggy. The next comfortable exit point is 90 minutes but for most of us carving an extra 90 minutes out of our day for sleeping is not practical.

Naps should be in addition to, not a substitute for, getting enough sleep at night (meaning 7–8 hours in most cases). But when you find your brainpower flagging, rather than struggling through 20 unproductive minutes, taking a short power nap may well be the answer.

Keep a swipe file

THE PRINCIPLE

Adapting what works is a worthwhile creative shortcut

People who work in advertising have what they call a 'swipe' file. That's a collection of ads that have been effective and that serve as inspiration.

Your swipe file should contain good ideas and examples from your field of work or interest and from other fields. It's from the latter that you are likely to get the best ideas that haven't been used in your field.

Things you might put into your swipe file include:

- clippings of newspaper and magazine articles
- print ads that catch your attention
- notes about radio and television ads that seem particularly effective
- videos that have gone viral on YouTube and other video-sharing sites
- photos you've taken of window displays or signs
- posts you've copied from blogs
- links to effective websites.

Get into the habit of looking for and recording everything around you that is inspirational, well designed and effective. As well as giving you raw material for adapting these to your own projects, it will put you in a positive, creative state of mind.

Balance your brain

THE PRINCIPLE

Balance between the hemispheres of your brain encourages calmness and creativity

Although the actual division isn't this neat, in general the left side of the brain is responsible for logic and linear thinking, while the right side is responsible for creativity and intuition. Certain physical actions are believed to be able to encourage better integration between the hemispheres, resulting in a greater state of emotional balance and creativity.

One such exercise, proposed by Hawkeen Training (www.navaching.com), is 'mind juggling'. Don't worry, you don't need circus-level skills – you use only one ball, like a tennis ball. Here's how you do it:

- Stand with your feet shoulder-width apart and your hands out in front of you as though you're holding a tray.
- Toss the ball from one hand to the other, looking towards the ceiling and then closing your eyes.
- Keep throwing the ball, letting it go about 4–6 inches high, at the rate of about once a second. If you drop the ball, just pick it up and resume.
- Keep going for about 10 minutes. When it feels easy, throw the ball higher or move your hands further apart so that there continues to be a bit of challenge to the process.

An even easier exercise is 'cross crawls'. To do it, stand and raise your right leg, bending at the knee, and bring your left hand over and touch the right knee. Then lower the right leg, raise the left leg, and touch it with your right hand. Basically you will be marching in place, touching each knee with the alternate hand. A few minutes should be enough, and to make it more challenging you can speed up the pace.

When you find yourself in a dull state of mind, try one or both of these and notice the difference (and ignore the weird looks you get from the other people in your office).

Website bonus

At www.CreativityNowOnline.com, click on the 'Creativity Now!' button. Bonus 8 is a video showing you how to do these two exercises and a couple of others.

Feed your brain

THE PRINCIPLE

What you eat affects your brain functions – for better and worse

As reported in *Psychology Today*, what you eat has a major effect on how well your brain functions: 'It's becoming pretty clear in research labs around the country that the right food, or the natural neurochemicals that they contain, can enhance mental capabilities – help you concentrate, tune sensorimotor skills, keep you motivated, magnify memory, speed reaction times, defuse stress, perhaps even prevent brain aging.'

For specific guidelines personal to you, consult your doctor or a nutritionist, but as a general guideline, here are some foods that may help you gain mental sharpness:

- Canola oil, walnut oil, salmon and sardines for their Omega-3 fatty acids.
- Eggs and skimmed milk for their choline content.
- Curries for the chemical curcumin.
- Cocoa and cranberries for their antioxidants.
- Coffee, for its stimulant effect. (However, it's not clear how much is too much. You'll get better results by sipping it over the course of the day rather than having several large cups at various points, and green tea may be a healthier alternative.)
- Fresh fruit for its glucose. (The actual fruit is preferable to juice because it contains fibre and is slower to break down in your system, therefore giving you more sustained energy.)
- Water: whether from the tap or bottled, you need water to stay hydrated and a good goal is to drink eight glasses of water over the course of a day.

It's also a good idea to avoid blood sugar spikes by eating smaller meals more frequently, and combining carbohydrates with protein (for instance, combine an egg with a piece of toast, or a serving of salmon with a potato). In the last few years, a low-glycemic diet has found favour, and you can find many books on the topic that give you the ratings of various types of food.

If you currently are eating too much fatty food, drinking lots of sugary soft drinks and consuming chocolate bars, crisps and other junk food, you may be doing a disservice to your brain as well as your body. Try changing your diet and notice the effect on your mood and your thinking.

Create a goals board

THE PRINCIPLE

Being reminded of what you want keeps you on the right course

Have you ever noticed that when you're in the market for a certain item, for example a washing machine, suddenly the world is full of magazine ads about washing machines, articles about washing machines, and even billboards featuring washing machines? And a week after you've bought a new one and the topic is no longer of interest to you, they all seem to disappear?

Of course, they don't really magically appear and disappear. The reason it seems that way is that for a brief time they are of particular relevance to you and that's when you notice them. Our mind draws us to the things we want or need in the moment and then screens them out when they are no longer important to us.

I'm guessing your creative goals are important to you. That's why it's vital that you keep them in mind. When you do, you'll automatically notice lots of relevant opportunities. However, it's surprisingly easy to be distracted from your goals. The demands of day-to-day living seem more important (and sometimes actually are more urgent). That's why it's not unusual to set a goal or make a resolution and to wake up some weeks or months later not having acted on them, and wonder whatever happened to your determination to make them happen.

An antidote to this is to create a goals board. This can be a physical item or a virtual one. To create a physical one, get a piece of white board, at least A2 size, ideally A1, and on it paste pictures, quotes, even physical objects, all of which represent your most important goal.

For a virtual version, create a file on your computer that includes similar images and keep it open most of the time so you are constantly reminded of it.

For aspiring novelists, the board might feature a bestseller list, photos of J. K. Rowling, Elmore Leonard or whoever they most admire.

For people who want to make their name in architecture, it might be pictures of the classical and modern buildings they admire.

For entrepreneurs, it might feature pictures of Sir Richard Branson and Steve Jobs and the cover of a magazine that they hope will someday feature their own story.

It doesn't matter what the pictures or objects are, as long as they have an impact on you. They should get you excited about your goal. If you start to get too used to your version of the board, keep adding to it and changing it with new items. Position the board somewhere you'll see it every day, so it can feed your desire, your determination and your creativity every time you look at it.

Join the League of Adventurers

THE PRINCIPLE

A spirit of adventure makes life enjoyable, creative and exciting

When we think of adventurers, we associate them with climbing mountains, sailing seas and exploring distant lands. However, we can have adventures in our own backyard – and in our own heads – if we remember to be curious, positive and creative.

I think that if you bought this book and have taken on board some of the methods in this part on dreaming, you are already an adventurer.

I'd like to make it official. If you'd like a personal, full-colour membership card admitting you to the League of Adventurers, send me an email with your name and postal address and I will be happy to send you one, no charge. Send the email to: **jurgenwolff@gmail.com**.

When you have received your card, if you like, take a picture of yourself with it, and I'll add it to our Gallery of Adventurers (see Website bonus, below).

While you wait for your card to arrive, venture into the next part – Originating – which will show you how to create an endless flow of exciting ideas to enrich your life and the lives of others.

Website bonus

At **www.CreativityNowOnline.com**, click on the 'Creativity Now!' button. Bonus 9 is a Gallery of Adventurers, including you if you send me a picture of yourself holding your official League of Adventurers membership card.

originating

2

Now it gets really exciting.

With your mind prepped to be in a creative mood, you're ready to learn methods for generating an endless flow of ideas.

In this part you'll find 25 ways to come up with new, exciting and innovative ideas on any topic.

When you've mastered a few of these, you'll be as creative as the average five-year-old child.

That's a good thing.

Follow the four brainstorming guidelines

THE PRINCIPLE

Brainstorming is more productive when you follow four simple guidelines

It may seem a paradox to set rules for thinking out of the box, but if you follow the four simple guidelines below, you'll find that your brainstorming sessions are more productive.

1 **Quantity counts.** During a session come up with as many ideas as you can, as quickly as you can. Nobel prizewinner Linus Pauling revealed the secret of his prodigious ability to generate breakthroughs: 'I have lots and lots and lots of ideas, and then I throw away the bad ones.' The key in that statement is 'lots and lots and lots of ideas'.

2 **No judging!** There will be a time to evaluate your ideas and throw away the bad ones, but the brainstorming session is not it. This is the hardest part of the process. We seem to be wired to respond critically as soon as a new idea appears. You need to make sure that you (or others, if you're doing this in a group) don't judge ideas as they come up. Judging includes not only critical comments, but also eye-rolling, tsking and shaking your head. Even if your immediate response to an idea is that it's impractical, too expensive or just plain stupid, hold off. If you're brainstorming in a group and there's judging going on, fine the offender a pound every time it happens. The proceeds can be used to buy snacks for the next session.

3 **Write down every idea.** Writing down some ideas and not others is a form of judging. If you're brainstorming in a group, it can be useful to have two scribes, each one writing down alternate ideas. Often the ideas fly too fast and furious for just one person to keep up. If you have that problem when brainstorming alone, then instead of writing down your ideas, use a tape recorder.

4 **Don't be afraid to build on other ideas – yours or someone else's.** Sometimes a small addition to or variation of an existing idea is what turns it into a real breakthrough.

If you keep these four guidelines in mind, your brainstorming sessions will be more likely to provide you with a full flow of ideas.

Website bonus

At **www.CreativityNowOnline.com**, click on the 'Creativity Now!' button. Bonus 10 is a downloadable poster featuring the four guidelines for effective brainstorming. You can print one out and put it on the wall of the room where you do your brainstorming.

Ask the ignorant

THE PRINCIPLE

People who don't know what they don't know sometimes know more than the people who know only what they know

When you know a lot about a topic, you may automatically block ideas that don't fit into the accepted rules about that field.

That's why so many breakthroughs in a particular discipline come from people who approach it from a different angle. It's also why Walt Disney's Imagineering Blue Sky programme hires young interns to spend the summer coming up with new ideas for attractions for the Disney theme parks.

Stanford University engineering professor Robert I. Sutton described it to the *Los Angeles Times* as bringing together 'people who know too much and people who know too little'.

When you want fresh ideas, here are some types of people you might consult:

- children
- the elderly
- people from a different culture (e.g. tourists from countries other than your own)
- people who work in a field totally different from your own.

The most important thing: don't dismiss their ideas as unworkable just because they've never been done before – that's exactly why they could be valuable. You will then bring your experience and knowledge to bear as well; and the combination of the two may be exactly what's needed for a breakthrough.

DEF

Try the opposite

THE PRINCIPLE

Thinking of the opposite of what's usually done may lead you to a practical solution

When we try to think of solutions to a challenge our first impulse is to return to the methods that have already been tried.

Instead, figure out the opposite of the way it's usually done. Then brainstorm how the opposite could be turned into something that works.

Example One: When the producers of the film *Gorillas in the Mist* were concerned about how they could possibly get gorillas in the wild to do all the things in the script, a young member of their staff suggested, 'Why not let the gorillas write the script?'

What she meant was that rather than making the gorillas fit what's in the script, shoot whatever they do naturally and then work the script around that. And that's what they did.

Example Two: You are opening a new store and you'd like to attract crowds. However, the press are not interested and it looks like nobody is going to show up.

The usual: Tell everybody.

The opposite: Keep it a secret.

Of course, if you literally keep it a secret, nobody will come. But if you brainstorm about secrets, and how appealing they are, you might hit upon the idea of writing a 'confidential' letter on the store's letterhead to your store manager, indicating that a famous person (let's say David Beckham) happens to be related to one of the salespeople and will be dropping by on opening day. Add that the manager must not tell anyone because the place might be mobbed.

You could make a hundred or so copies of this letter and happen to leave them 'accidentally', one by one, in public places. When people start ringing to ask if it's true, the store manager might say 'No comment.'

Of course, on the day, to avoid being attacked by the crowd you might want to have a David Beckham lookalike drive by in a limo and have him wave. (This actually happened, but the details have been changed – for instance, it wasn't David Beckham – to protect the guilty.)

Your turn. Summarise the problem on a piece of paper. In a column down the left side of the page, jot down three or four usual things people do to try to solve the problem. Down a centre column, jot down the opposite of each of the usual methods. And in a right-hand column, write down what practical ideas come out of thinking of the opposite. Even though it's no longer really the opposite, it's highly likely it will be more productive than the usual methods that were your starting points.

Do a future interview

THE PRINCIPLE

Being interviewed about having reached your goal gives you clues as to how to get there

The following exercise will take 10–15 minutes of undisturbed time, so turn off your phone or go to a quiet place where no one will interrupt the process. Also have a pen and paper ready or, even better, a tape or digital recorder.

When you're ready, I'd like you to imagine a time in the future when you have achieved your most cherished goal. Take a moment to daydream about what that will feel like.

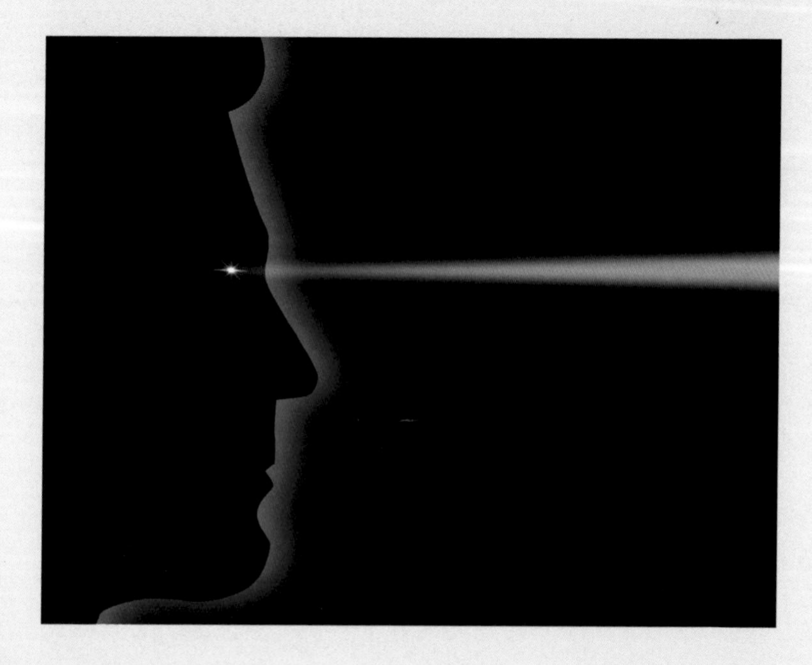

Now imagine that someone, perhaps a reporter or a friend you haven't seen for a while, wants to ask you some questions about how you achieved this terrific accomplishment. Choose someone you would feel comfortable with.

Imagine this person asking you the following seven questions. For each one, make sure you get into that state where you are imagining you have already reached the goal, then imagine yourself answering the question, and then jot down the essence of your answer or speak it into the recorder. You may need to take a moment to get back into the right imagined state each time you deal with a new question. Ready? Here are your questions:

1 What's the best thing about having achieved your goal?

2 What motivated you to go for it – why was it important to you?

3 What was the very first step you took to move towards it?

4 What was one early obstacle and how did you overcome it?

5 Who helped you along the way?

6 What was the most important factor in helping you reach your goal?

7 What advice would you give to someone else with the same goal, who is just starting out?

When you are done, bring yourself fully back to the present moment and review what you've written or dictated. Often you will find that this process has brought up interesting and useful information that you didn't even know you knew.

Force a word association

THE PRINCIPLE

Forcing a connection between your challenge and an unrelated word yields new ideas

This method is one of the most popular brainstorming tools, for a very good reason: it's simple, you can do it alone or in a group and it works.

You begin with a list of random words. You can pick them out of a newspaper or magazine, and the words can be anything: an object, a place, a type of person, an emotion, an action. Write down at least 20 of them in a vertical column on the left side of a page. For our example, my list includes:

Bedlam

Fish

Soloist

Door

Kidnapper

Joke

Then pick one creative challenge where you need some fresh ideas. Next, write a summary of the issue across the top of the page. For example, let's say you're a parent who is trying to motivate his or her teenage son to study more.

The method is to see what ideas come up when you combine that challenge with each word on your list. Let's see how it works.

What could be the connection between the teenager who needs to study and 'Bedlam' (which was a notorious insane asylum that allowed tourists to come and watch the inmates for the visitors' amusement)? It's important to remember that the forced association is designed to start a flow of thoughts – you don't have to stay with the word itself. So, in the case of Bedlam, we might think of the humiliation of the patients. Perhaps you could tell your son that unless he studies more, you will show up at school every day to walk home with him (no teenager could imagine greater humiliation than that ...).

Studying combined with 'Fish' might remind you that consuming certain types of fish helps brain power. And that might motivate you to check your teenager's diet to make sure he's getting enough Omega-3 fatty acids.

Studying combined with 'Soloist' might remind you that when he's studying alone he tends to get distracted. So maybe it would be worthwhile getting him a tutor once a week or, to combine this with humiliation, study along with him.

Give it a try yourself with a real challenge. Start with my list just to get a taste of how easy and useful this method can be. Then generate some random word lists of your own, so you have them ready whenever you want to generate new ideas quickly. You can employ similar methods with pictures by forcing an association between your topic and random images from magazines.

When you have a good idea – keep going!

THE PRINCIPLE

Settling for the first good idea you have stops you from having a better one

It's tempting to stop as soon as you come up with a good idea. However, if you keep going, you might come up with an even better one.

One way to make sure you don't stop is to set yourself a minimum number of ideas to generate in a given time. Set yourself a high standard – remember, they don't all have to be good ideas (anyway, you're not judging at this point, remember?) and write down everything as quickly as you can.

A good target is 50 ideas in 15 minutes. The pressure to keep coming up with more ideas helps you gain momentum. And even if idea number 10 seems like the perfect solution, carry on.

When you're ready to evaluate the ideas, instead of choosing just one, choose at least three finalists, even if you're already pretty sure that one of them is the best by far.

Then have an additional brainstorming session of at least 5 minutes for each of the three final ideas, trying to come up with variations that could make it better.

Finally, pick the best ideas from those sessions, and evaluate the three solutions again – you may find that now a different one comes out ahead.

Start with the end

THE PRINCIPLE

One way to come up with good solutions is to start at the end and work your way backward

One powerful method for developing a product or service is to start with the end – what you want it to be, in as much detail as possible – and work backward.

When imagining the outcome, don't worry about how you'll get there, that's for later. For now, just describe the final result as fully as you can.

As an example, let's say your goal is to be recognised as a top speaker in the field of management. What are some of the outcomes you'd like to achieve? They could include:

- being booked to speak at major conferences (for a hefty fee)
- being an expert guest on radio and TV shows when they discuss your specialist topic
- being profiled in the major UK management trade publications
- being paid to consult with top managers to coach them to deliver their own presentations.

Now you can start working backward from each of these outcomes. Before you are booked to speak at major conferences, what else would have to happen? Usually, you'd be booked to speak at paying lower-end events where you could prove your skill and be noticed by agents from speakers' bureaux.

Then work backward from that step. Before you are booked for those kinds of events, you might hone your speaking ability by speaking for free for charities and civic organisations.

And before that, you might need to gain confidence and skill by joining Toastmasters, where you can practise and get constructive feedback.

When you've worked your way back from each of your desired outcomes to where you are today, you will have a complete roadmap for how to get from here to where you want to be.

Website bonus

At **www.CreativityNowOnline.com**, click on the 'Creativity Now!' button. Bonus 11 is a map of how I started with the end-vision of an information product I sell on the internet and worked my way back, right to the beginning step.

Apply your why, who, what, where and when questions

THE PRINCIPLE

Asking questions is a great way to explore any problem – and discover solutions

In the first part I talked about the power of questions to reawaken the sense of curiosity we all had as children. In the course of originating ideas, you can also use this questioning process in a more targeted way.

One approach is to start with how things are done at the moment and question that with the persistence of Socrates (who must have been really annoying to be around). For instance, let's say we're trying to come up with a new approach to business cards. We might ask:

- **Why** paper cards? That leads us to consider what else they could be made of: cloth, metal, wood, leaves (remember, we're not judging at this point!), stone.
- **Who** should be on your card? Normally it's you, but who else could be on it? Satisfied customers with testimonials? Your family? Your parents? Your dog? The people who most inspire you? The bully who gave you the determination to succeed?
- **What** information should it contain? In addition to, or in place of, your contact information, could it contain a puzzle? A quote? A question for the person you give it to? A discount coupon?
- **Where** do you use business cards? Yes, at networking events and meetings, but where else could you give them out or leave them? At the library or in a book store, you could tuck a card into all the books that relate to your product or service. You could attach them to small chocolate bars and give them away at a convention.
- **When** is the best time to give someone your card? The usual thing is to give it to someone the moment you meet them, or when you're about to wind up your chat. When else could you do it? You could hand out half a card and say you'll post them the rest (assuming you collect their card, so you know where to send it). If the half you give them has an intriguing question on it, the other half could have the answer. Or the first half might have an image that looks like one thing but when it's matched with the other half, the image turns into something else. If the point is to make you memorable, there are lots of possibilities.

When you have gone through all the questions, look over all the ideas you have generated and see which ones go together. You may find that by giving the current approach the third-degree, you have invented a fresh and exciting new one.

Have a Trendstorming session

THE PRINCIPLE

Relating the important trends of the time to your product or service leads to improvements

Our priorities, likes and dislikes change all the time, and so do political and economic developments. Anticipating these is an important way to thrive at all times, rather than just reacting (or, even worse, reacting too late). Entire industries, like the automobile sector, have courted disaster by ignoring such changes.

You can avoid a similar fate by having regular brainstorming sessions in which you consider what the trends are and how they might affect you. Note that we're talking about trends, which are medium- to long-term developments, not fads that vanish as quickly as they pop up.

In your session, first list all the trends that you have observed yourself or that have been covered extensively in the media. These might include the baby-boom generation's desire to stay as youthful as possible, the drive towards cleaner energy and the obesity epidemic.

These trends are already in mid-flow and you should have considered already how best to respond to them, but if you haven't, now is the time.

It's tempting to dismiss some of these as not being relevant to you. For instance, the obesity epidemic obviously impacts clothing manufacturers, health clubs and insurance companies. But when you take a closer look, you see that it also affects all kinds of other areas: airlines use more fuel because the passengers are heavier; hospitals need larger ambulances to transport extra-large patients; and makers of school furniture need to design the next generation of chairs for heavier kids. Take the time to go more deeply into whether and how such trends may affect you.

Next, make a list of trends that are not yet well established but that you and others sense might be about to take off. This is more difficult because they will not yet be covered by the mainstream media.

Many social trends start with young people, so it's important to keep an eye on what they're wearing, what they're talking about, what online sites they are making newly popular, and so forth.

Some trends come from other countries and cultures. To spot these, it helps to read newspapers and magazines from other countries. A great place to do this is **www.thepaperboy.com**. There you can access newspapers by country. For example, I just had a look at the *Afghan Daily* and the *Copenhagen Post*. Some of the newspapers, like these two, are in English; others are in the national language. Pay attention to the ads as well as the stories.

Another useful tool is **www.google.com/trends**. It shows you the top terms people are searching for every day on Google. Some of these reflect fads, but if you see certain terms coming up consistently over a period of weeks and months, they may point to a trend.

Trendstorming once a month or so, and seeing how you can apply what you've spotted, can put you ahead of the curve instead of behind it.

Use mind maps

THE PRINCIPLE

Using a graphic representation allows you to explore any idea more easily

Creativity guru Tony Buzan made mind maps popular and has written several books on how to draw them. The basic format is an oval or square in the centre of a piece of paper in which you write your main topic. Then draw lines radiating outward from the central shape, and on each line write a word or phrase that relates to it. You add sub-branches to those lines to go into more detail.

Below I've drawn a mind map exploring some different methods I might use to add interest to a workshop I'm going to give. Starting at the top right (about the one o'clock position) and going clockwise, I draw some branches, one for each main idea. These are props, multi-media elements, guest speakers, activities for the participants and surprises.

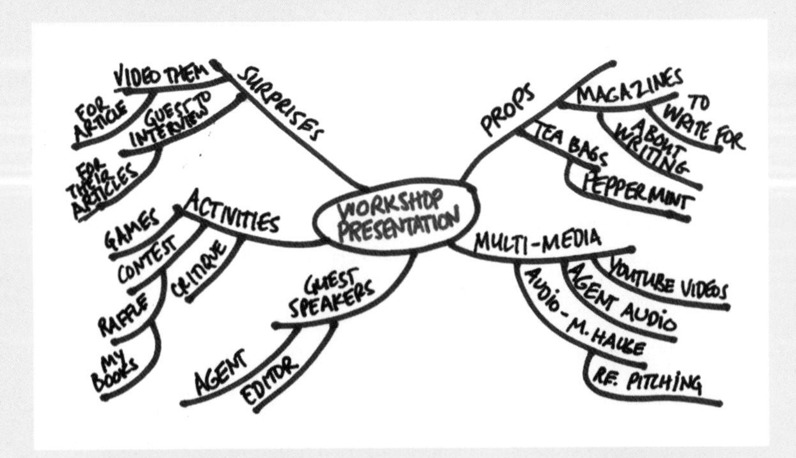

Then I go back to each of the branches and draw extensions for each idea I have for that topic. This workshop is about how to make money by writing, so the first props that come to mind are magazines (and you'll see that I've added further branches to indicate the two types of magazine I have in mind – those about writing, and those that use freelance writers). The next one is tea bags. Sometimes after lunch I hand out peppermint tea bags and have the participants sniff them because the smell of peppermint is supposed to revive your energy.

The next branch is 'multi-media', and the ideas are to project some YouTube videos of writers talking about their craft, and to play two audio interviews I have done in the past, one with an agent, the other with a friend who is an expert on pitching ideas.

Branch three is the notion of asking some guest speakers to take part, and the two who probably would be of most interest would be an agent and an editor.

For the fourth branch, 'activities', I might build in some games and a contest or raffle with my books as prizes. Another possibility is to ask participants to bring in something they've written themselves, and do a critique of it.

The final branch is for surprises – me videotaping the participants and showing them how to turn that into an article that could be sold, or inviting an interesting guest for them to interview and turn that into an article.

One advantage of mind maps is that you can fit a lot of information onto one page. It becomes easier to notice possible connections and combinations. For instance, if I have an agent as a guest speaker, instead of getting him or her to give a talk, I might make it an interview conducted by the students, and have each of them write a brief article that I would then critique.

Mind maps are also an excellent way to record input during a group brainstorming session. Do it on a very large sheet of paper and have two people doing the writing so no ideas are lost.

You can draw mind maps by hand but there are also many software programs, both free and for sale, that do the same thing.

Website bonus

At **www.CreativityNowOnline.com**, Bonus 12 is an article about some of the best mind-mapping software programs available and where to get them.

Try Freewriting

THE PRINCIPLE

Writing quickly about a topic or question reveals information that may have been hidden

Freewriting is writing whatever comes to your mind for a set period of time. Begin by writing a concise description of the challenge or problem you would like to explore. Then set a timer for five minutes and start writing whatever comes to mind about the issue.

When the first five minutes are up, take a short break (just a minute or two) and review what you have written. Circle the three words or phrases that seem most interesting or important. If you're not sure, let your intuition guide you. Then decide which of the three actually is the most important and write that at the top of a new sheet of paper.

Set the timer and repeat the process – write whatever comes to mind about the word or phrase you chose.

When the second five-minute period is up, do the same thing one more time: circle the three most meaningful or interesting or important words or phrases, pick one, and do a final five minutes of writing. Again circle the three most important phrases or sentences and then give some thought to how they illuminate the original challenge or topic.

Often you will find that this process reveals new ways of looking at your original topic, or new ideas for how to handle it.

Let's look at an example, in brief form. I had one of my coaching clients do the exercise, and his topic was 'How to overcome procrastination'. I won't include his full exercise here, but the three phrases he circled from his first five-minute session were:

- → Fear of certain technology-related tasks
- → Reluctance to give up anything I'm interested in
- → Stuck on a few key things

As the topic for his second five minutes, he chose the last one. After another five minutes of speed writing, the three things he circled were:

- → Getting my office and files, etc. cleaned up and organised
- → Reaching my fitness goals
- → I feel like I'm always taking 3 steps forward and 2.75 steps back

For his final session, he again chose the last phrase. What was interesting about his freewriting was that it was quite emotional. Here are the three things he circled from that session:

- → This wakes up some kind of childish frustration of having no power
- → I have control over how I spend my time
- → I want to stop sapping my own power!

The insight he got from the process was that with his procrastination, he is actually perpetuating something negative from his childhood. This made him quite angry – and determined to stop doing this.

It's not unusual for freewriting to reveal the deeper issues relating to a challenge that you are facing. When you are ready to give it a try, remember these four guidelines:

1. Keep writing! If you get stuck, just write the challenge over and over until something new pops into your mind.
2. Don't censor yourself. You will not be showing this to anybody else.
3. If you feel you're getting close to something useful but need more time, keep repeating the exercise until you get there.
4. If five minutes per exercise doesn't seem enough, try working with ten-minute periods.

You may discover the key to behaviours that are holding you back – and how to change them so you can surge forward.

Challenge all assumptions

THE PRINCIPLE

Assumptions about your challenge may be limiting your creativity

Every challenge has behind it a set of assumptions that seem so obvious that most people never think to challenge them. At one point it seemed ridiculous that a metal tube full of people would ever be able to fly through the air. Or how about the notion that you can type a word into a computer and in under one second up will pop millions of pages of material about that topic – crazy, right? As you can tell from these examples, breakthroughs overturn assumptions.

To challenge the assumptions around your challenge, you first have to be aware of what they are. Start the process by making a list of what 'everybody knows to be true' about the topic (which could be a problem, an invention, a service or just about anything else).

Let's say the challenge is that you've written a book and you'd like to get it published. Some of the typical assumptions are:

- You need an agent to bring your manuscript to the attention of publishers.
- Publishers generally don't look at unsolicited manuscripts.
- Even if your book is published, it will be difficult to get attention for it in the media if you're not famous.

As a writing coach and lecturer, I know that these kinds of assumptions stop a lot of people from attempting to write a book, even when they have a terrific idea. So let's at the same time challenge each assumption and brainstorm some alternatives.

Do you really need an agent to bring your manuscript to the attention of a publisher? Who else might have a connection to a publisher? How about your dentist, solicitor, gardener, university lecturer or insurance agent? The 'six degrees' notion that we are no more than six links from reaching anybody has been proven – can you make it work for you? What would happen if you started asking everybody you deal with whether they have any connections to a publisher?

Next, what might make a publisher more receptive to considering your manuscript (other than a personal connection)? If you wrote an article on your topic for a major newspaper or magazine, would that be a way to get their attention? If you researched the major publishing executives using the resources of the internet, do you think you might find one who has some specific interest in your topic? For instance, if your book is about growing up poor in a small town, which publisher has a similar background? If your book is about improving one's golf game, which publisher is an avid golfer?

Finally, is it really impossible to get media attention for your book even though you're not well known? Perhaps you can take advantage of the fact that the media love stunts. One author of fantasy fiction arranged for a 'dragon foetus' to be discovered (with the help of a company that made it out of wax and an accomplice who pretended that he found it in the effects of his grandfather, who supposedly worked at the Natural History Museum). The author's book, *Unearthly History*, had been rejected by 36 literary agents and 7 publishers, but after the stunt Allistair Mitchell published it himself and got an exclusive distribution deal with Waterstone's and a three-book deal with the American branch of HarperCollins for £100,000.

As you can see, the rewards of questioning assumptions can be considerable!

Imagine someone else's solution

THE PRINCIPLE

Imagining how a well-known innovator (or company) would attack the problem can lead to new ideas

When you have a challenge or want to come up with a new idea, try imagining how a well-known innovator like Walt Disney or an innovative company like Apple or Virgin would handle it. Decide what are the two or three distinguishing features of that person or company, and consider how to apply those to your problem.

To see how this works, let's assume that your challenge is finding ways to motivate people to recycle more.

The Walt Disney solution would be family-friendly and fun. Could you develop a game that makes recycling enjoyable and maybe competitive? The Disney company promote their movies with McDonald's. Could you do the same and get a restaurant chain to offer coupons for the kids who are most successful coming up with recycling schemes for their family? Or get them to sponsor a recycling day once a year?

Apple would find an innovative and stylish solution. Could you collaborate with a company that would design attractive, streamlined recycling containers? Could the existing recycling bins be fitted with a unit that says 'Thank you!' each time someone deposits something? Or could charity shops be given tokens for iTunes downloads to hand out to people who bring in a certain amount of clothing or other goods?

Virgin would find a brash solution and launch it with a stunt featuring Richard Branson doing something daring. Can you think of a stunt to draw attention to the cause of recycling? Could you find a celebrity to front it? If not Sir Richard, maybe a television personality or an actor from one of the popular soaps?

Of course, you don't have to limit yourself to my examples. Make your own list of people and companies you consider innovative. List the attributes of each, and then go down the list and brainstorm how those attributes could be applied to your challenge, invention or idea.

Vary the attributes

THE PRINCIPLE

Start with the idea or object or service as it is, then vary its attributes to find a better way

If you'd like to come up with a better version of a product or service that already exists, one way is to try varying its attributes. Among the many variations you can try are:

- Make it larger.
- Make it smaller.
- Make it simpler (subtract functions).
- Make it more complicated (add functions).
- Make it more frequent or less frequent.
- Make it more colourful.
- Make it more appealing to young people/older people.
- Make it easier to access.
- Make it more exclusive.

Let's try a few of these with the example of an alarm clock:

- You could make it **larger** so it can easily be seen across the room, and to turn it off the person has to actually get up, so there's no danger of oversleeping.
- You could make it **smaller** so it can be clipped to the pocket of a pair of pyjamas or to a pillow.
- You could **add** a tape recorder function on which you record your loved one's voice saying good morning – nice to take with you when you're away on business trips.

- → You could make it **more appealing to young people** by making it in the form of an animal that jumps up and down when it rings.
- → You could make it **more appealing to (some) older people** by having the alarm function as a voice that gives a different Zen quote every day of the month.
- → You could make it **easier to access** by allowing it to be controlled by your voice.
- → You could make it **more exclusive** by creating the clock's face from limited-edition prints by Salvador Dali or other artists.

When you've listed all the possibilities, you might find interesting combinations. For instance, since kids are notoriously hard to wake up, a big clock that you have to cross the room to turn off could also contain a recorder so it plays the message, 'Get up now! Don't make me come to your room!'

Staying true to the notion that most new things are just variations on what already exists, this method opens up almost endless possibilities for your creativity.

Teach your problem

THE PRINCIPLE

When you describe how you do a problem, you also learn how to stop doing it

This technique is for any habit or behaviour you'd like to change. The best way to do it is to get a partner who will listen and take notes while you teach them to do the same thing, in detail.

For example, you might give a lesson in how to be late, how to over-eat, how to make sure you never exercise, how to procrastinate or just about anything else. The other person takes notes and, if necessary, prompts you with questions to make sure you go into adequate detail.

When you get the notes back, all you have to do is the opposite of everything your partner has written down.

I used this method to overcome my former habit of being late. Would you like to learn how to be late? I can help! Here are just a few of my proven methods:

- Have no clocks in the bathroom so when you're shaving or doing your hair it will be easy to lose track of time.
- Just before you leave the house, check your email one more time and answer any urgent or interesting messages.
- Assume that public transport will be on time or that it will be easy to find a taxi or that traffic will be light.
- If the phone rings as you're on your way out, run back and take the call even though your answer machine is on.

I know lots more ways to be late, but that gives you the idea of how the process works. And, yes, now I do have a clock in the bathroom, I do assume that public transport will be running late (I take along reading material so I have something to do in case I do arrive for a meeting early), and I no longer do 'just one last check' of my emails.

If you don't have a willing partner for this exercise, you can dictate your lesson into a tape recorder and then transcribe what you've said, but it's much more fun with a live listener. By making it a game, it's funny and enjoyable, but yields seriously useful information at the same time.

Which of your habits will you teach – and change – first?

Make 1 + 1 equal 3

THE PRINCIPLE

Collaboration can give results that are greater than the sum of the parts

Many, if not most, important breakthroughs are the result of teamwork. Even if one person led the effort, it's only in the arts that geniuses tend to work by themselves, and even there most of them will admit to being heavily influenced by someone else.

The mistake most of us make when looking for someone to work with is seeking someone who is a lot like us. After all, people tend to like those they perceive to be like themselves. That's fine for finding someone to go to the pub with, but exactly the wrong strategy for finding a collaborator.

Professor Scott Page of the University of Michigan, the author of *The Difference: How the Power of Diversity Creates Better Groups, Teams, Schools, and Societies*, said: 'Watson plus Crick were far more impressive than either in isolation.' He also pointed out that on a far larger scale, Silicon Valley's breadth of bright engineers from different academic disciplines and from around the world out-innovates other technology hotspots with equal brainpower but less diversity.

The best collaborator has strengths that you lack, and vice versa. This sometimes also means that you will have different personalities and interests and may not naturally be the best of friends, but that shouldn't matter.

If you want to find a collaborator, consider someone whose background and worldviews are different from your own. This could mean differences in gender, race, ethnicity, physical capabilities, culture, geographical location and sexual orientation, as well as education or training.

With the advent of the internet, it has become possible to collaborate easily with people halfway around the world whom you may never actually meet.

The same principle applies to situations in which you are not collaborating but looking for someone to hire for certain functions. The section 'Outsource' in Part 3 will give you some tips on how to find those people.

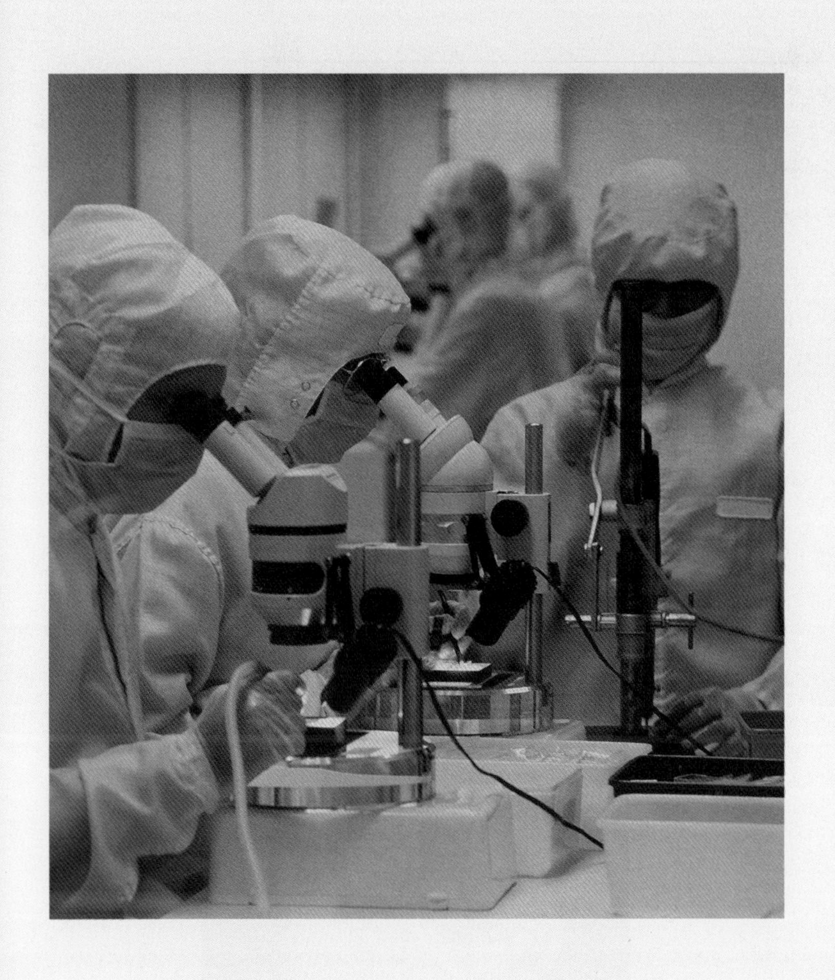

Summon your Originator alter ego

THE PRINCIPLE

Vividly evoking a time when you were very creative makes it easier to be creative again

In my book, *Focus: Use the Power of Targeted Thinking* (Pearson), I introduced the notion of alter egos. It's based on the idea that all of us have lots of sub-personalities that come out at different times.

For instance, some people are quite relaxed when meeting with someone one-to-one but nervous when they have to address a group. Similarly, you might be assertive in one situation but more timid in another.

Most of the time we leave it to chance which of our sub-personalities (or, as I call them, alter egos) is in charge, but there's a way to make it a choice. That way you can be sure that the task at hand will be handled most appropriately, effectively and efficiently.

Having a 'curious kid' alter ego can be great when you're exploring ideas. However, if you put the curious kid in charge of cleaning your garage, it's not going to work out too well. The kid will find a stack of magazines or a box of mementoes, get engrossed, and four hours later nothing will have been dealt with. For that job, you should consider making your Attila the Hun alter ego the boss.

I'm sure you also have an 'Originator' alter ego – the part of yourself that comes up with lots of ideas. Here's how to get into that state whenever you want:

- Remember a time when you experienced that state. It may have been recently or you may need to go all the way back to when you were a child.
- In your imagination, vividly recall what the world looked like when you were in that state, anything you said to yourself or that others said to you, and especially what it felt like in your body.
- When that feeling is really strong, make a gesture like pressing your thumb and forefinger together (in Neuro-Linguistic Programming, this is called an 'anchor').
- Practise doing this a few separate times. You are establishing a connection between those feelings and the gesture.
- The next time you want to get ideas flowing, make the gesture and you should notice yourself returning to the Originator alter ego state. If the feeling starts to weaken, or you are distracted and sense you're losing that state, just make the gesture again.

Stay in that state until you've finished your brainstorming, then decide what you want to do next and what kind of alter ego would best serve you in that task. With practice, you can have a whole team of alter egos at your beck and call.

Combine

THE PRINCIPLE

Combining two ideas or things can lead to something new

One way that new things emerge is by combining the essence of two existing things. For example:

Phone + copier = fax machine

Home movies + internet = YouTube

Video game + exercise = Nintendo Wii

Bicycle + carriage = rickshaw

One you may be less familiar with: Sleeping bag + sheets = thin 'body envelopes' you take with you when you travel so you don't have to be exposed to possibly dirty sheets or beds in hotels.

There are two ways you can use this combining principle to come up with ideas for new products or services. One is to combine two elements that are already related in some way. This will lead to ideas that may not be radical or hugely innovative but can still be useful.

For instance, we could combine two styles of books, such as gardening and cookbooks that come in a binder with removable pages. The result might be a set of laminated cards that you can take outside with you and refer to when planting or pruning certain kinds of plants.

Or we might combine a T-shirt with shorts and come up with a one-piece boiler suit with short sleeves and cut-off legs (no, I wouldn't look good in one, either).

The other option is to combine two elements that are very different. For example, we could combine gardening with aeroplanes, and come up with hanging planters in the shape of aeroplanes or a Zeppelin.

Or we could combine a T-shirt with a traffic light, and create a T-shirt that you can wear to clubs and control so it lights up green when you see someone you want to speak to, or red if there is someone approaching you whom you'd rather not speak to.

Try it both ways. Take a product or service you'd like to make more interesting or appealing and make two lists. One is for things that are in the same general realm as what you're starting with; the other is a list of things that have no apparent relationship to it.

Then spend at least 15 minutes brainstorming with each list and see which one gives you better ideas.

Learn from nature

THE PRINCIPLE

Nature makes a great model for new ideas

It's sometimes called 'biomimicry': innovation inspired by nature. One of the best-known examples is Velcro, which was based on the grappling hooks of seeds, but there are plenty of others:

- In order to develop new adhesives, scientists are studying how geckos are able to stick so well to walls.
- The sea cucumber, which normally is soft and pliable but can secrete chemicals to stiffen its skin, has inspired the invention of new plastics that go hard to soft when exposed to water.
- Engineers at Speedo studied shark skin to come up with a new swimsuit (it was worn by most of the medal winners in the 2008 Olympics, including Michael Phelps).
- The quiet operation of the Japanese bullet trains is due to noise-dampening designs mimicking the features of owls and the beaks of kingfishers.

You don't need to be a scientist or engineer to copy nature, nor are the lessons of nature restricted to high-tech applications. As well as more literal versions of nature, we can use nature symbolically.

For example, consider the caterpillar that emerges from its cocoon and transforms into a butterfly. The model here is a transformation after a period of development. How might we apply this concept?

For my book, *Your Writing Coach* (published by Nicholas Brealey), I include a code word at the end of each chapter. When you have read the chapter (that's the development period), you can go to the website (**www.yourwritingcoach.com**) and type in the code word, which unlocks a series of bonuses, including video interviews with the co-creator of the TV series *24*, a book agent and others (this is the transformation into a different source of information).

Another example: if you have an online or offline retail business, how can you let your relationship with customers transform after they have spent a certain amount of money with you? Perhaps at that point they become VIP members of your club and get access to exclusive offers, or they become eligible for a monthly prize draw.

If you want to be inspired by nature, start with a list of things from nature that intrigue you. Then try relating each of these, literally or as a metaphor, to the problem you are trying to solve. You may find that Mother Nature knows best.

Match your interests and your skills

THE PRINCIPLE

Randomly matching your interests with your skills can give you new ideas for how to make money

This method is great when you want to come up with new ways to make money doing something you enjoy. It was first proposed by Fredric Lehrman in his *Prosperity Consciousness* audio programme (Nightingale-Conant). He calls it 'Prosperity Scrabble'. Here's how to play.

Cut up sheets of paper into squares about an inch wide, so you have 100 of them.

On one set of 50, write things that you really enjoy doing. These could be activities like gardening, drawing, listening to music, swimming, watching television, making your own wine, reading thrillers – anything and everything you can think of that gives you pleasure.

On the other set of 50, write down your skills. For example, maybe you are good at cooking, talking to children, doing accounts, helping friends with their problems or keeping fit. Again, write down as many as possible, one per small piece of paper. In some cases, the same thing will appear in both sets.

Turn them all over and mix them up (but keeping the two sets separate). Then pick one from each set and brainstorm how you could combine them (if you happen to draw two that are the same, pick another).

Another way to do this is just to make two numbered lists, one for what you enjoy, the other for what you do well, and then randomly match a number from one with a number from the other.

I'll give you an example from my own two lists. From the 'What I like to do' cards I picked 'going to the theatre' and from the 'What I do well' I picked 'podcasting'. (In case you're not familiar with podcasting, it's creating an audio or video programme to distribute over the internet, including via iTunes – you'll find one on my website, **www.CreativityNowOnline.com**.)

If I wanted to find a new way of making money by combining these two, one option would be to create a podcast about theatre. I live in London, very near the West End, so I'm close to the action. And there is worldwide interest in the West End theatre world, so it's not too hard to imagine either finding a sponsor for such a podcast, or selling advertising time on it once it attracts a large enough audience.

Another combination that I came up with was 'watching television' and 'teaching'. How could I combine these to make money? Possibly I could assess which are the most popular TV shows at the moment, and develop a workshop around the topic. For instance, at the time I'm writing this, *Dragons' Den* is very popular. I happen to have a lot of experience in pitching ideas for TV and film, which is pretty similar to pitching ideas for business. So offering a pitching workshop for aspiring entrepreneurs, using the hook of *Dragons' Den* in my title or publicity (while, of course, being clear that I have no official connection to the TV show), might be a good idea.

Give it a try and you may discover all kinds of combinations that can be the starting points for profitable new ventures.

Fish in a different pond

THE PRINCIPLE

Targeting a different audience for what you already do may reveal lucrative new markets

Many times everyone who offers a particular product or service is chasing the same set of customers. Often the best way to surge ahead of the competition is to figure out how to slant the product or service to a different audience.

The Nintendo Wii is a great example of this. At a time when many video games were chasing the fanboys who love shoot-em-ups, the folks at Nintendo realised that there was a whole new potential audience out there for games that didn't involve killing anybody. The motion-control element was also a new way to interact, and the upshot was a success that put competitors in the shade.

You may find an untapped audience by appealing to different groups according to various criteria including:

1 **Age groups.** Can you adapt it to appeal to children, teenagers, young adults, the middle-aged, the elderly?
2 **Gender.** Can you adapt it so that it appeals to a different gender?
3 **Geographic location.** Can you offer it to people who live in other areas, perhaps by using the internet?
4 **Occupation.** Can you figure out how to make it useful for people in other occupations?
5 **Hobbies.** Can you adapt it to people with different interests?
6 **Relationship status.** Can it be adapted to appeal more to singles? Or to people in a committed relationship? Or to people newly engaged or recently divorced? Or to new parents?

7 **Values.** Can you make it appeal to those especially concerned with protecting the environment? Or those worried about their personal safety? Or people wanting to be seen as high-status?

Let's take the straightforward example of financial planners who are struggling to find new business. Using the list above, they might come up with these ideas:

- Specialise in helping the elderly take charge of their finances.
- Work with recent graduates who are new to the world of work.
- Specialise in working with people who are self-employed or, even more specifically, with freelancers.
- Target young parents to help them to plan for their children's futures.
- Target customers who are especially interested in finding ethical investments.

Once you decide what kinds of individuals or groups might be a new target audience for you, you need to figure out how to market to them effectively. Here my book *Marketing for Entrepreneurs* (Pearson) will be helpful.

Obviously not every product or service lends itself to every one of these variations, but you might surprise yourself with how many you can generate. When everybody is fishing in the same pond – find another pond!

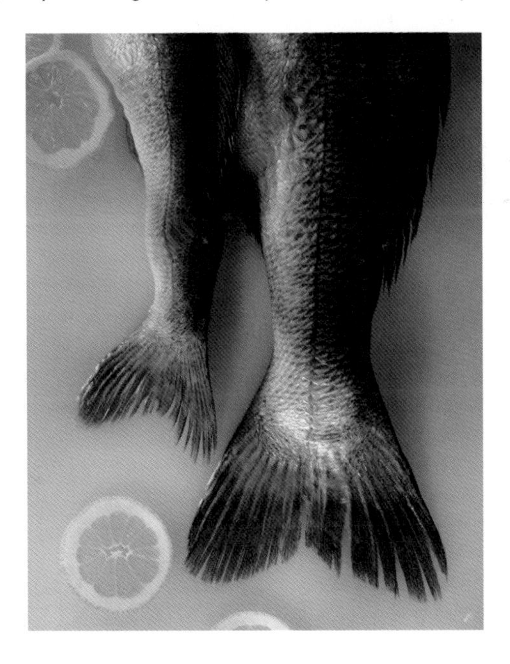

Repurpose

THE PRINCIPLE

Finding a new way to use an existing idea in a different context yields new value

Repurposing could also be called recycling – not for ecological reasons, but for profit. For instance, if you have written a non-fiction book, you could use basically the same information to create:

- an audio book
- a series of podcasts
- a live workshop
- a series of teleseminars
- an educational video series or multi-media product.

Naturally, you would need to ensure that there are no contractual issues with your publisher regarding exploiting the same information in a way that might compete directly with the book. In fact, most of these additional uses tend to be complementary. People who attend a workshop or teleseminar or hear a podcast or see a video series will be more likely to want to buy the book.

Another example: a friend of mine is a children's entertainer called 'Mr Squash'. How could he repurpose his puppet show? Some ideas that come to mind:

- Make a video of his basic show and sell it at the parties where he entertains – kids love to see the same things again and again.
- Record the actual performance on audio, including the sound of the kids singing along, and sell that on CDs to the parents of the kids who attended.
- Make a storybook out of his show and sell that as a present that the hosts can give to the kids who attend their child's birthday party.

As you can see from these two examples, the way to repurpose what you do is to consider all the additional media you might employ:

- audio
- video
- print
- live events, including workshops, lectures and teleseminars.

How many ways can you generate to make more money by extending what you already know and do?

Steal their methods

THE PRINCIPLE

Applying the methods of a successful enterprise to your own challenge leads to success

There are all kinds of successful enterprises that you can use as models even if they are not in your field. In fact, it's better if they are NOT in your field, otherwise you will just be copying what they do too literally.

I first came up with this idea when someone who had visited my writing blog (**www.timetowrite.blogs.com**) emailed me asking for help coming up with ideas for a screenplay. This is what I advised:

> *'Take a look at the storylines of movies you have really enjoyed and that have been successful. Consider how you could substitute different elements to build your story. For instance,* E.T. *is about a lonely little boy who tries to shield an alien from the authorities and help him get back home, and along the way the boy learns the meaning of true friendship.*
>
> *If you were to transplant that to a different era, who might be a fugitive? Maybe a criminal, or someone with dangerous political ideas. Who might befriend him? It could be a servant or an outcast of some kind. Who would be the bad guys after the fugitive? How might the life of the person trying to help him or her be endangered?*
>
> *This might seem like plagiarism, but by the time you have finished adapting it to your era and circumstances, it will come out very differently.'*

Another example: one thing Disneyland does well is to minimise the annoyance that goes with waiting to get to the front of the queue at their rides. They tell you how long it'll be before you arrive (and they always overestimate this time so you'll be pleasantly surprised when it takes less). They distract you with video screens, live performers and music. They construct the queues so they are constantly moving, giving you a sense of continual progress.

If you have any kind of business in which the customers have to queue, Disneyland would be a great model.

In summary, follow these three steps:

1. Identify an outstanding business not in exactly the same field.
2. Make a list of the outstanding methods this business uses.
3. Brainstorm how to transfer this to what you do.

When you apply their innovative methods to your realm, you'll be lauded for your originality (how you got there will be our little secret).

Website bonus

At www.CreativityNowOnline.com, Bonus 13 is a video about some of the methods used by casinos in Las Vegas to keep you gambling.

Eliminate creative blocks

THE PRINCIPLE

Creative blocks are obstacles you can overcome – not the end of the road

On our most creative days we don't even feel what we're doing is work. We're in a state of flow and time passes without us noticing.

On the worst days, nothing's flowing. Our brains feel empty and even the effort of trying to come up with a bad idea, much less a good one, is too much.

Fortunately there are a variety of ways to overcome creative blocks. In this section you'll discover half a dozen approaches – not the usual 'take a break' or 'go for a change of scenery' tips you've heard a million times, but methods that are themselves creative and therefore more likely to ignite the rest of your creativity.

1 Interview the block

When you imagine your creative block, what image or sound or feeling comes to mind? Maybe it's a wall or a growling lion or a feeling in the pit of your stomach.

Imagine a dialogue in which you ask what it's trying to do for you. As with the inner critic, assume it has a positive intention. Often it's trying to protect you, perhaps because what you are creating is bringing up difficult memories, or you fear it might upset someone, or you worry that nobody will value it.

Once you know the intention of the block, you can create the conditions that make the creative process safer. For instance, let's say you find yourself blocked from finishing a painting and your interview with the block reveals that it's worried that the painting will not be good enough. You can make a deal with yourself: you'll finish it, put it out of sight for two weeks, and then return to it to decide whether it's any good. If not, you'll discard it – or paint over it.

2 Look for the source of the problem further back

When we get stuck in the middle of a creative project often it's because we didn't lay the groundwork for it properly.

For instance, if you are plotting a novel or screenplay and get stuck in the middle, go back to the first section and make sure you've complicated your characters' lives enough there to give you material to work with in the middle.

In you run out of steam halfway through crafting a presentation, go back to the audience's starting points: how much do they already know about your topic, in which aspects are they most interested, what do they expect to hear, what would (pleasantly) surprise them?

Even in a painting, getting stuck may come from being so eager to get to your brushes that you didn't plan the composition carefully enough.

Getting unstuck is just a matter of finding the right approach to handle the specific issue that's causing the problem – and often the source is somewhere earlier. Go there and you're likely to find the solution.

3 Make the right comparisons

Sometimes the work of people more skilled can be inspirational, but at other times it can make us think, 'I'll never be that good, why bother?'

There will always be somebody worse than you and somebody better than you. Others will judge whether or not they like what you have done. Sometimes nobody likes something when it first comes out and later it becomes a cult hit or even hugely popular (Van Gogh's paintings, for instance). Other times something is a big hit when it first comes out but is forgotten a few years later.

You have no control over these things. You just have to get on with your work. If you want to make comparisons, here are three that are useful:

> ***'Compared to what else I could be doing, is this the project for which I have the most passion?'***

> ***'Compared to what I've done in the past, am I applying to this project what I've learned?'***

> ***'Compared to my dreams, does this project reach high enough?'***

These are the comparisons that can spur you to getting back to your creative work.

4 Try a different medium

The novelist Janet Evanovich once told an interviewer how she got started writing. Initially she was a painter and one day, while drawing with her daughter, she realised that whenever she drew or painted she was telling a story in her mind about what she was portraying. She decided to write down some of those stories, and that led to a successful career first as a writer of romance novels and then of crime fiction.

If you're a stuck writer try telling your story with simple drawings first, even if you have no particular talent for art. If a specific character is eluding you, draw them and see what new ideas come up.

On the other hand, if your creativity normally take a visual form try using words instead.

Using a different part of your creativity takes the focus off the block and allows fresh ideas to emerge.

5 Give up

Give up – but not on the entire project, just on the part that's giving you the trouble at the moment. We're taught to start at the beginning and work through to the end, but sometimes the beginning is so daunting that it's hard to get started. No problem – work on another part of the project.

For example, if you're trying to come up with a presentation and you have no idea how to start, instead create your big finish or an important moment in the middle. Then figure out what might come just before or after that bit and keep going. By the time you've got everything else done, the perfect opening will probably pop out at you.

6 Make a choice

Sometimes it's the inability to choose between two or more options that stops a person like a deer in the headlights. What if you choose the wrong turn of the plot, the wrong colour, the wrong way to present your great idea to the people whose investment you want?

There are three points to remember that can relieve your anxiety:

1 These choices don't have to be permanent. Do commit to the ones that seem right and follow them through all the way. Don't jump back and forth. But recognise that if, when you are done and have given it your best shot, it turns out you chose unwisely, you can go back and make changes or adjustments. There is always the option of a new draft, a different colour scheme, a new audience.

2 Often the choice is not as important as how you execute that choice. In other words, it's about how well you write whichever version of the story you choose, or the confidence with which you present the idea more than the exact words.

3 Your anxiety will decrease once you get more deeply into the process. Recognise it for what it is – a version of first-date jitters. Go past it and you may find yourself in a beautiful relationship.

Stay calm

Above all, don't panic. If you are walking along and find your path blocked by a tree, you don't give up your journey or blame yourself. You analyse whether to go around it, over it or maybe even under it, and then you continue. With the six methods you've just learned you can do the same for a creative block. It's a temporary obstacle, not a creative death sentence.

Believe in goosebumps

THE PRINCIPLE

For other people to get excited by something, first* you *have to be excited by it

Someone asked the great Quincy Jones how he knew that a song or album was going to be a hit. He said some people in the music business believe in using focus groups and other research strategies, but his approach is different. He said:

> ***'I believe in goosebumps.'***

He knows that if something you create gives you goosebumps, the chances are that it'll do the same for others.

Before you move forward into the next part, which will give you methods for turning your ideas into realities, I suggest that you write down the answers to the following questions for each project you pursue. Then take them with you for the rest of your journey with that idea or project.

What do I want the user to *feel* when they experience what I have created?

Much of the time we hope to create a certain kind of experience for the people who use our product or service, and often the most important part of that is emotional. What emotions do you want to evoke?

What parts of the project are most exciting for me personally?

These elements usually are the quirkiest or most individual and therefore often the first to be eliminated because they don't fit an established pattern or norm. However, they also may be exactly the elements that could lead you to a breakthrough.

What unique strengths do I bring to this project?

Focus on your strengths, not your weaknesses, and figure out how to allow the project to reflect those strengths.

Where does my intuition lead me in regard to this project?

This is part of the 'goosebumps' aspect of what you're setting out to do. What hunches and feelings do you have about what you can accomplish with this project?

What are ten reasons why I CAN do this project successfully?

Usually our first impulse upon having a new idea is to come up with ten reasons why we probably couldn't do it, and if we run short, helpful friends and relatives are happy to chime in with their negativity. Consciously listing ten reasons why success is possible helps to counteract this habit.

When the critics review this project, what kind of raves will they give it?

Be as specific as possible – even sit down and write the review yourself.

Keep a journal for each project you undertake, and make these questions and answers the first section you write. The journey will not always be smooth – looking back on how and why the project gave you goosebumps will help you along the way.

Me? I get goosebumps imagining the great ideas you will generate with the help of this book.

applying

lying

3

This is the part other books on creativity are missing.

The part about how you take that bright, shining idea and turn it into something real: planning, staying focused, collaborating, testing, revising, taking initial rejection in your stride and masterfully managing your time.

The hard part.

The part that earns you money, glory, or both.

Let's go to work ...

Summon your Action Man or Woman alter ego

THE PRINCIPLE

To turn your dream into the reality you need to change your mental state

In the last part, I described how to summon the 'Originator' alter ego, the part of yourself that is great at brainstorming and thinking out of the box. That is the state perfect for generating lots of new ideas. But if you remain in that state when you move on to turn one of those dreams into reality, probably you will never accomplish what you set out to do.

If you have a history of starting things but never quite finishing them, it may be because you stay in the dreamer state too long. When dreamers encounter an obstacle, their minds tend to wander to other things they could do. They are attracted by the bright, shiny lure of new ideas and distracted from the task at hand. The result is a trail of half-finished projects and a sense of frustration.

The solution is to switch to the Action Man or Action Woman alter ego when you want to turn your idea into something tangible. The process is the same as when you summoned the Originator alter ego. Here are the five steps:

1. Remember a time when you were decisive and focused on getting things done. It may have been recently or you may need to go all the way back to when you were a child.

2. In your imagination, vividly recall what the world looked like when you were in that state, anything you said to yourself or that others said to you and especially what it felt like in your body.

3. When that feeling is really strong, make a gesture like pressing your thumb and a finger together. Use a different combination than you used for the Originator alter ego. For example, maybe you used your thumb and forefinger that time. This time use your thumb and little finger.

4. Practise doing this a few separate times. You are establishing a connection between those feelings and the gesture.

5. The next time you want to take specific, focused action, make the gesture and you should notice yourself returning to the Action Man or Action Woman alter ego state. If the feeling starts to weaken or you are distracted and feel you're losing that state, just make the gesture again.

Stay in that state until you've finished your working session, then decide what you want to do next and what kind of alter ego would best serve you in that task. As I mentioned before, with practice you can have a whole team of alter egos at your beck and call.

Create an action map

THE PRINCIPLE

Creating a diagram of what you need to do focuses your activity

In the previous part, I suggested using a mind map to bring out all your thoughts about an idea you want to develop. At that point, having ideas all over the place is fine, it's a part of expanding your thinking. However, now that you are taking action, what you need is an action map.

An action map uses the same basic structure as a mind map but instead of ideas you are mapping tasks, and instead of a random order you are using a chronological order.

The sample action map below illustrates the process. The project name is in the oval in the centre. In this case, the project is to rewrite my ebook on Time Management. I've gone through the stage of brainstorming how to make it even more useful, and now it's time to implement those ideas.

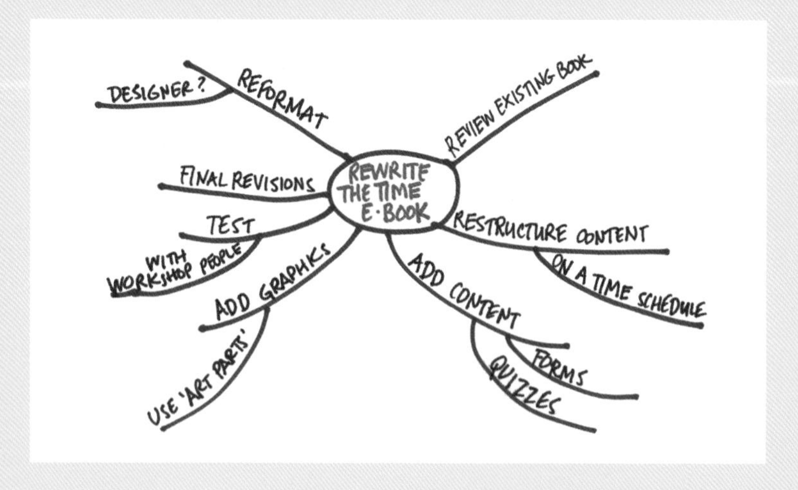

Again, we start at the one o'clock position. The first task is to review the existing book again to get my mind focused on the topic. Then we move clockwise to the next task, which is restructuring the content. Coming off that branch is the sub-branch that says 'on a time schedule'. What I mean by this is that I plan to put the content into a structure that readers can use step by step, week by week, to reclaim their time.

The next branch is 'add content' and the sub-branches indicate that two types of new content are: (i) forms readers can fill out to help them apply the principles to their own life; and (ii) quizzes that help them figure out what they need to do.

The next branch is 'add graphics' because I plan to add more visuals. The sub-branch, 'use Art Parts', relates to the name of a set of graphics that I own.

Next is 'test', because I always like to make sure that everything that I offer has actually worked not only for me but also for others. I have a workshop coming up and will offer test versions of the new materials to the participants.

Next is 'final revisions', which will incorporate any feedback from my test group, and the last step is to 'reformat' the ebook. I've indicated that I'm not sure yet whether I will do this myself or get a graphic designer to do it.

One of the key benefits of using an action map is that it forces you to think through the entire process. If some steps are not clear yet, jot down what you think they will be, but add a question mark. You can always quickly add to or redraw the action map as new information comes up. Typically, I will redraw my action map at least three times over the course of a project.

Having thought the process through, you end up with a concise, easy-to-read plan for achieving it. You can use a highlighter pen to cross off each step as you finish it.

When you have finished the project, keep the action map because it may come in handy if you want to do a similar project in the future. Instead of reinventing the wheel, you will start with an approach that has already shown itself to be successful.

To get, ask

THE PRINCIPLE

When you need help implementing a project, the way to get is to ask

Being a pioneer can be lonely. If you look closely at the people who have had a significant impact in their fields, you'll find it's very seldom they did it alone. Don't be afraid to ask for help – even from unusual sources.

Advertising legend George Lois dared to ask. In fact, that's how he saved MTV. After its first year of operation, it was failing because cable operators in the US refused to carry it. He created commercials that ended with the announcer saying, 'If you don't get MTV where you live, call your cable operator and say…' and then Mick Jagger (or Pete Townshend or Pat Benatar) shouted into a telephone: 'I WANT MY MTV!!!'

Lois told me, 'In each city, thousands called moments after viewing the commercial and screamed for their MTV! Within months, MTV was in 80 per cent of all households.'

On a separate piece of paper write down what you want. Then brainstorm who might be able to help you get it. Here are some possible choices (hint: think what you can give as well as what you want to get):

- customers (or customers once-removed, as with the MTV example)
- suppliers
- colleagues
- family members
- competitors (can you find common ground for a win–win?)
- someone famous who uses your product or service
- friends
- businesses that have similar customers but are not your competitors
- the media.

Who is most likely to be able to help you? List them by name, position or description.

Finally, brainstorm how you can **motivate** them to do it (George Lois did it by using rock superstars). Here are some good motivators (to be used ethically, of course):

- payment
- flattery – how can helping you make them look good?
- win–win deals
- just asking
- reciprocal favours
- recognition (certificates, public thanks)
- association with something worthy
- association with celebrities.

Go back to your list of possible helpers. How could you motivate each of them? With the right help, almost anything is possible. Start asking!

Give them a taste

THE PRINCIPLE

Sometimes to sell something, you've got to give a sample

When you're doing something different it can be difficult for others to get on board because they can't quite imagine this new product, service or idea. If you need their support in order to complete your project, one strategy is to give them a taste. It works for ice cream parlours, and it can work for you.

It also worked for Eric Idle. According to *The Times*, the other surviving members of the Monty Python group were reluctant to let him use their material for his 'Spamalot' musical – until he gave them a sample. He said:

> ***'That was the hardest thing – to persuade them that this was something that would go well. We played them the song, "The Song That Goes Like This", and they cracked up. That was the secret of it.'***

The show played on Broadway and in the West End of London.

To employ this method, answer these questions:

- Who do you need to win over?
- What is their biggest doubt or objection?
- What part of your project is most likely to overcome those doubts?
- How can you create that part as a sample? Would a prototype work? A drawing? A video? A simulation?

Once they've had a taste, if it's good they're likely to buy.

To sell, pre-sell

THE PRINCIPLE

Preparing your audience helps make them receptive

You may think that perfecting your product or service before approaching your target audience (which might be customers or your boss) is the best strategy, but often it is much more effective to prepare them in advance. If you can also give them a sense of participation, they will be even more receptive.

The fact behind this principle is that however much we like to think of ourselves as forward-looking, innovative risk-takers, most people are scared of change. And if you have come up with something new, it will involve change. That's why most innovations are resisted. A blogger who identifies himself only as John (at **www.indefinitearticles.com**) summarised the five stages of innovation as follows (I'm paraphrasing them here):

1. **Denial.** Saying the new thing will never work.
2. **Anger** that some people seem to be embracing the change.
3. **Bargaining.** Trying to figure out a way to accept the change without actually changing.
4. **Sadness** because you feel too old or not tuned in enough to cope with the change.
5. **Acceptance.**

I would add a sixth step:

6. **Pretending** that you were for it all along.

If you've ever tried to introduce change within a large corporation, these steps may seem dispiritingly familiar. Here are three ways you can prepare your target audience for the great new thing you are developing:

1. **Make them more aware of the problem** that your innovation is designed to solve. For instance, for my Time Management programme, I could send my mailing list a survey of ten questions about their time issues. Do they find it frustrating to deal with email? Do they have any 'time vampires' in their lives – people who drain their energy and their time with trivial matters? Do they procrastinate? At this point I'm just gathering data, not trying to sell anything. But when I follow up with an offer of a product that addresses these issues, my target customers will have been sensitised to their need for it.
2. **Ask them for input.** I could also send my target customers a questionnaire asking them what features they would like to see in a programme on Time Management. Again, at this stage it's not about selling. But if I later offer them a product that clearly addresses the issues they have raised, they will be more likely to buy.
3. **Ask them for feedback.** Give them a beta version of your product or allow them to sample your service and ask them what could be improved. When you later offer them the actual product and show that you have incorporated their ideas, they will feel a sense of ownership which, again, will incline them to buy.

While these strategies will help you to sell, they are also extremely valuable in their own right – they help ensure you are designing a product or service that meets the actual needs of your potential customers, not just your perception of those needs. These two benefits make this a crucial part of turning your idea into profitable reality.

Use OPM

THE PRINCIPLE

If you're short of funds, use other people's money (OPM)

There is an even more literal version of pre-selling, namely selling a product before it exists. Artist Karen Sperling did this. She's an expert at using a software program called Painter to transform photos into paintings. She has taught this internationally and has contributed to a number of books. When she decided to write and self-publish her own book on the subject, she asked people to order and pay for it in advance, and to wait six months to get it.

It's a clever approach because it instantly gave her an idea of how many potential customers there were for the book and of course it meant she could use their money to produce the product.

If you use this approach and you don't get enough people paying, you can refund the money and nobody has lost anything.

A friend of mine, Chris Jones, used a similar approach to fund the production of his award-winning short film, *Gone Fishing*. He wanted to produce a film that would show off his talents as a director so he offered people an Associate Producer credit on this film if they donated £50 towards its production. Their names would be featured (in very small print) at the end of the film. He managed to raise more than £15,000 and produced a heart-warming film starring Bill Paterson, who has appeared in hundreds of TV shows and films. It qualified for the long-list for the Oscars. Those of us who put in our money knew we'd never get it back, it was just a way to support an aspiring film-maker and have a bit of fun too.

Raising money this way works best if you have a way of easily contacting potential customers who already know and trust you. If you don't have your own list, it may be possible to collaborate with someone who does, in exchange for a commission or a barter of services.

So, if you find that your quest to turn your idea into reality is foundering due to a lack of money, consider how you can use other people's!

Declare a MAD

THE PRINCIPLE

A concentrated day of working only on your project creates momentum

On any given day, it's probably rare that you have only one thing to work on. Being able to juggle several projects at a time is a necessary skill, but sometimes when we divide our working day into small units it feels like none of our projects are moving forward at a satisfactory rate.

One solution is scheduling a MAD – Massive Action Day. It simply means one day when you put aside everything else and focus on only one project. This requires you to turn off your phone, your email, the television, and cancel any social engagements. If necessary, put an automatic message on your email service letting people know that you will be responding the next day. Screen any phone calls and only return ones that involve the possibility of imminent loss of life.

Start your MAD with all the resources you will need at hand. This could include files, office supplies, lists of phone numbers, software, etc. You don't want to spend the first half of your day looking for materials.

Set a timer, whether on your computer desktop or just a kitchen timer, for 45 minutes and work for that period without stopping. When the buzzer goes off, take 5 minutes to refresh yourself with a drink of water, a walk around the office or a few simple exercises, plus a toilet break if you need one. Then set the timer for another 45 minutes and repeat. After every three sessions, give yourself a 15-minute break. Stick with healthy, non-stodgy food so you don't feel lethargic. If it helps, consume reasonable amounts of caffeine during the early part of the day.

When you have put in 8 hours on this schedule, you will find you have accomplished more work than you normally get done most weeks. You may also feel very tired, but it'll be a good kind of tired.

Use a MAD whenever you want to gain momentum. You may even find that you want to turn one day each week into a Massive Action Day – if you do, you will astound others (and yourself) with your new productivity.

I regularly run online Massive Action Days. If you'd like to attend one, you can sign up at the website, www.CreativityNowOnline.com.

Use the Pareto Principle

THE PRINCIPLE

20 per cent of what you do gives you 80 per cent of the value

The Pareto Principle is also known as the 80/20 rule or the Law of the Vital Few. It was derived from the observation by Italian economist Vilfredo Pareto that 80 per cent of the land in Italy was owned by only 20 per cent of the population. It has since been extended to many other situations and seems to be reflected in our mundane experience – for instance, the likelihood that you wear 20 per cent of your clothing 80 per cent of the time.

The application that concerns us here is the notion that 20 per cent of what you do gives you 80 per cent of the value. This is borne out by the observation by time management experts that most people spend no more than 90 minutes of their 8-hour days actually working.

The obvious conclusion is that if you can figure out what that most valuable 20 per cent is, and do more of it, you will get lots more value. In order to have time to devote to that 20 per cent, of course you have to eliminate some of the not-so-valuable 80 per cent. You can try this now: list the five things you do that bring in the most money. (Naturally, money is not the only indicator of value, but it's the one we will focus on for the moment.)

Now list five things you do at work that take up your time but don't actually yield much value. Some of these may be essential even if they don't provide direct value. For instance, filing doesn't pay off directly but if you never do it, that will eventually affect your ability to do efficiently the things that do pay off. The idea is not necessarily to get rid of these tasks (unless you can) but to delegate them so you have more time to spend on the things that do greatly add to your income.

Which of the five things that don't add so much value could you delegate? To whom? (If you're not sure, this part's discussion of outsourcing may help you.) If you didn't have to spend time on those, which of the top value-producing tasks could you spend more time on? What do you think the outcome of that would be?

You can apply this to a specific project, too. What's the most crucial 20 per cent that you need to get done? What can or should you delegate? For example, in the discussion in the section on action maps, one of the tasks I included was reformatting an ebook and I listed the possibility of having a graphic designer do this instead of me. Most likely a designer would do it faster and better than I could, and that would free up my time to spend on activities that are in my top 20 per cent.

If you're intrigued by the Pareto Principle, you can test it out by applying it even for just one day. Figure out what are the highest-value tasks you can tackle that day and devote yourself to those only. That's different from a Massive Action Day because you can work on several projects during the course of the day, but in each case only on the aspects that create the most value. At the end of the day, assess your results. I predict that you'll become a fan of the 80/20 rule.

Website bonus

At www.CreativityNowOnline.com, click on the 'Creativity Now!' button. Bonus 14 shows you how to supercharge your productivity by applying the 80/20 rule to your to-do list.

Test a prototype

THE PRINCIPLE

You don't need a finished version to get valuable input

If you're creating something complex, it can be devastating to put in all of the work only to discover through testing or audience reaction that it has serious flaws. In many cases it's possible to avoid this by creating a prototype or virtual version, or a version that is unfinished but complete enough to get feedback.

For example, in the case of non-fiction books, publishers don't need to see a complete manuscript in order to decide whether or not to commission the work. Usually they prefer to see a proposal that contains the table of contents, a brief summary of each chapter, and one or two sample chapters, as well as information about competing titles and how you would help market the book. That way they can make suggestions for changes before you actually write the bulk of the book.

In engineering, prototyping is the norm. A device is built and tested and adjusted or redesigned as necessary before going into production.

Similarly, software is released in a beta version to allow early users to find the bugs that need to be fixed before the program is distributed widely.

Different projects will lend themselves to different ways to achieve a similar result. Here are five approaches to choose from:

1 Create a partially finished version but describe the rest of it well enough that the target group can give you feedback. The book proposal is an example of this.

2 Create a virtual version that shows the functions of the final product before you actually build it in the real world. This might mean getting a 3D graphic of it that people can interact with on a computer.

3 Take something that already exists and (on the actual item or virtually) add the functions that you think will make your version superior and test it. For instance, if you have an idea for a superior toaster, you may be able

to take an existing one and rig it to add your new functions before going to the expense of building a totally new one.

4 Test a smaller version. For example, rather than opening your own store, it may be possible to open a mini-version within a mall or even within another store to test customer response.

5 Test it in limited numbers. For instance, you can have a few copies of a brochure or catalogue printed digitally and get feedback before you print thousands of copies.

When you have decided which of these approaches best matches your innovation, you will have a formula for saving time and money on the way to your breakthrough product or service.

Piggyback

THE PRINCIPLE

Sometimes riding piggyback is easier than going it alone

The odds are that whatever your idea, it's an improved version of something that already exists. If that 'something' is successful, it may be a good idea to find a way to piggyback onto it rather than trying to come up with something totally new. This kind of piggybacking is an advantage both in the creation and the marketing processes. In the former, it can save you work. In the latter, you will find that people generally are quicker to accept (and buy) something that relates to what they already know.

An example from my own experience: I am developing innovative ways to manage your time better, but I appreciate the work that has been done by David Allen, author of *Get It Done* and several other books that have had huge, worldwide success. In my materials, I acknowledge his work and make it clear that the methods I offer are designed to make his approach even more effective (without implying, of course, that he endorses or has any official connection with my work).

Here's the four-step process for this kind of piggybacking:

1. List the best features of your most successful competition.
2. Brainstorm what value you can add to what they already offer.
3. Design your product or service to deliver that value.
4. Market your offering. You can decide whether to openly acknowledge the competition (for instance, with an ad that promotes your coffee shop as 'Beyond Starbucks') or to make no reference to it.

There is also another form of piggybacking, where you collaborate with a person or company that is already successful. In publishing, one example of this is the *Guerrilla Marketing* books. Jay Conrad Levinson wrote the original and now works with experts in different fields to co-author books on guerrilla marketing in their area (for instance, *Guerrilla Marketing for Consultants* and *Guerrilla Marketing for Job Hunters*).

If someone already has an established name in your field, he or she may be willing to collaborate and share the proceeds. If they bring credibility or access to the customers you are targeting, a share of the proceeds of that collaboration may yield more than 100 per cent of what you'd earn by going it alone.

Website bonus

At www.CreativityNowOnline.com, click on the 'Creativity Now!' button. Bonus 15 is a look at how you and I might piggyback on projects relating to creativity and productivity.

Outsource

THE PRINCIPLE

Get others to do what you don't do well

The internet has totally transformed the process of outsourcing. Although many people still think of the term solely in the context of call centres, these days it's easy to find people all over the world eager to take on the tasks you don't want to or can't do yourself. And they'll do it for a lot less than you're likely to pay locally.

Outsourcing fits well with the 80/20 principle that we covered earlier in this part. It makes sense to delegate the tasks that you don't do well or that don't represent the greatest value you can give. My list of things that I don't like and/or don't do very well includes:

- anything to do with accounts
- networking in person
- selling in person
- website creation
- filing.

Your list may well look totally different, but no matter what you dislike doing, there will be somebody out there who does enjoy it and will do it for you. Yes, it will cost you some money but it will also free up your time to earn money doing what you do (and like) best.

A few tasks, like filing, can be done only by someone who actually is present, but most can be done over the internet. There are hundreds of services where you can list what you want done and get people around the world to bid on it. One of the main ones is **www.elance.com**. The skills offered there include computer programming, writing and translation, design and multi-media, sales and marketing, administrative support, engineering and manufacturing, finance and management, and more. Some of the suppliers are individuals, others are companies. They could be in the UK, the USA, India, Egypt or anywhere else around the world.

You register and pick the category of help you want. Then you list your job and your fee range (for instance, between $50 and $500) and state for how long a period you want to accept bids. During that time, various people will offer to do the work for a specific sum. You can see their portfolio or references and also how much work they have previously done through the site and how their clients rated their work.

You can choose to award the assignment at any time and put the fee into an escrow account. If the task has several stages, you can release the fee in instalments as each stage is accomplished.

When you're done, you release the rest of the funds and rate the service you received. The task can be a one-off or it can be an ongoing service such as administrative support.

I've gone into detail about Elance because their procedure is similar to that of most other such services, and there are lots to choose from. They include RentACoder.com, HireMyMom.com and Guru.com.

The bottom line: people all over the world are anxious to help you turn your ideas into innovative and lucrative projects and for pay that won't break the bank.

Keep an Ideas Box

THE PRINCIPLE

While focusing on the project at hand, have a way to capture other ideas

One question I get asked a lot – and I'm guessing you do, too – is: 'Where do you get all your ideas?' Sometimes I say there's an ideas store in a basement in Soho.

The question always amuses me because for most creative people having enough ideas is not a problem. Having enough time to realise those ideas is the problem.

However, our tendency to have lots of ideas can sometimes become a trap. It can easily take our attention away from the project that should be getting most of our energy at that point. Especially when things aren't going so well, the thought of jumping to a new project is very tempting. At the same time, we don't want to be so totally absorbed with the current project that we let great new ideas get away.

The solution is an Ideas Box. This is simply a box, or a box file, or a folder in which you store ideas for future use. Whenever you have a new idea that is not relevant to your current project, jot it down on a piece of paper or an index card and drop it into your Ideas Box. If you're having a lot of ideas about a particular project, give it its own box.

When I read her wonderful book, *The Creative Habit*, I discovered that choreographer Twyla Tharp does something similar. She starts every dance with a box labelled with the project name and then drops into it everything that has anything to do with her research for that work. This could include notebooks, CDs, news clippings, videotapes, and so forth.

The only difference is that I'm suggesting creating such a box *before* you start working on the project formally, as a way to capture ideas.

When you finish your current project, you can go through the contents of your Ideas Box and decide which of the many notions should be next to be turned into an exciting reality.

Create a loyalty card

THE PRINCIPLE

Working step by step towards a reward keeps you motivated

Yes, ideally the work should be its own reward. But we've all experienced that blah feeling in the middle of a project when it has become hard work, things aren't falling into place in the way we'd hoped and the finish line is still a long way off.

One common recommendation for keeping yourself motivated is to reward yourself for reaching milestones along the way. The problem with this is that for little steps, the rewards tend to be so small that often we don't bother; and for big steps the reward is so far off that it's not very motivating.

A way around this is to adapt an idea commonly used by coffee shops and restaurants: the loyalty card. That's a little card you carry and that gets stamped or punched every time you buy something. When you've purchased ten coffees, for instance, you get a free one.

You can use an index card or even the back of a business card for your own version. At the top of the card write the milestone that you want to reach. For instance, if you're trying to write a book, maybe it's finishing the first chapter. Or if you're getting organised, maybe it's finishing the filing that has piled up.

At the bottom of the card write the reward you will be giving yourself. Maybe it's going to the cinema or out to dinner, or buying a book.

Decide how many daily steps the task might take. Ideally it would be between six and ten. If it's fewer than six or more than ten, adjust the scope of the task. Draw a small square to represent each step.

Every day that you accomplish a step towards this milestone, put a check mark in one of the boxes. When they have all been marked, you get the reward.

By the way, this is also a terrific tool to use with children: every ten times they have done some chore, or achieved a good score on their school tests or assignments, they get a little prize.

Using this kind of card yourself makes you 'loyal' to the idea of achieving your creative goals – and that's even better than a free large cappuccino!

Give it a personality

THE PRINCIPLE

Whatever you create will have a personality – make sure it's the one you want

Your brand is simply the impression people have when they think of your product or service. Every brand has a personality, for instance:

Apple = cool and sexy

Tesco = good value

Harrods = posh

You need to think about your project's personality while you are creating it. The personality needs to be an intrinsic part of it, not something that marketers and advertisers tack on later, whether or not it really fits.

When the American company Dave's Gourmet created a line of spicy sauces, they decided to go for the extreme. They concocted the hottest hot sauce ever sold and called it 'Dave's Insanity Sauce'. Their motto became, 'Snacks for an insane world.'

At the other end of the personality spectrum is the UK company Innocent Drinks, which produces a line of smoothies and juices. It projects a kind and – well – innocent image.

All kinds of factors go into a product's personality – colour, shape, size, ease of function, kind of function, the sound it makes, what it reminds people of, how rough or smooth it is, how light or heavy, and so on.

With a service, the factors include how easy it is to understand, what part of your problems it addresses, what you associate with it, how closely it aligns with other services you like to use (or which may have negative associations) and the surroundings within which it is delivered. For instance, the atmosphere of a dentist's waiting room heavily influences our experience.

As you develop your product or service from its original idea, consider the following questions:

- If this were a person, what is the one adjective you would use to describe it?
- Is that the personality you wish it to have? If not, what would you prefer?
- What, if anything, do you need to do to give it even more of the desired personality? This could involve the basic design, the packaging, or both.

When you have a prototype or sample ready, ask that first question of everybody who is exposed to your product or service.

Do they see it the same way? If not, what is giving them a different impression?

A person with a great personality is always popular. Keep making adjustments until your product or service has the kind of desirable personality that's likely to make it popular in the marketplace.

Keep it simple

THE PRINCIPLE

Keep your eye on the core functions of what you create

The deeper you get into the process of creating your project, the easier it is to go off on a tangent. One of the most seductive tangents is to keep adding new functions and bells and whistles.

This is what I call the 'Wouldn't it be cool?' trap. You're creating something and suddenly you have an idea for an element you could add. 'Wouldn't it be cool if this also ...?' you say to yourself, and tack on something else. This happens a lot with software, and often this 'features bloat' ends up slowing down the key functions that are all most users care about.

Sometimes the temptation to add things is an effort to appeal to a wider group of potential customers. For instance, maybe you start with a product that would make life easier for teachers. That gives you a huge potential target market. But then suddenly you have an idea how to add another element that would make it useful for nurses, too.

Great idea, right?

Wrong!

There's an old saying that if you try to please everybody, you end up pleasing nobody. The more diffuse your product or service, the less intensely it will appeal to the original target group. That's not to say, of course, that you couldn't eventually come out with a version of your product targeted specifically to nurses, but for now you'd be wise to keep focused on the original intention.

These three questions will help you to stay on course:

- Who is the primary customer for my project?
- What is the ONE main benefit they will get from it?
- To give them that one main benefit, what features does it need to have?

I'm emphasising the idea of one main benefit because 'benefit bloat' is another trap. As consumers, we are suspicious of products that promise too much. Figure out the one big challenge your potential customers have and make them aware that your product or service will solve it.

The more you know about your field and the deeper you get into your project, the more likely it is that you will make it more complex than it needs to be. Write these words on a Post-it note and put it where you can see it every day:

KEEP IT SIMPLE!

Ready, fire, aim!

THE PRINCIPLE

If you wait until the conditions are right, you'll never move forward

In my workshops and coaching I've met a lot of people who have a great idea but have never done anything with it. When I ask them why, the answer is almost always a version of, 'Because the conditions aren't right.'

The conditions that aren't right vary a lot. The person hasn't had time to do all the research he needs to, or she doesn't have enough money, or he doesn't have enough time, or the economy is bad right now, or, or, or …

These are not conditions; these are excuses.

Making something that changes the world, even in a small way, is hard. Making excuses is easy. That's why most people do the latter instead of the former. Now is a good time to switch sides.

The saying 'Ready, fire, aim!' acknowledges that we seldom have all the information we need or the ideal conditions. But if we move forward and try something, the real world will give us feedback. If we are off target, we adjust and try again. The most famous example of this is Thomas Edison and the number of filaments he went through before he found one that could be used for his light bulb. But actually this process is one that almost every business goes through on the way to success.

One example of a person who needed to learn this concept was an acquaintance who had an idea for a historical novel. Every time I ran into her over several years I'd ask how it was coming along. 'I'm still doing the research,' she said each time. She felt she had to become an expert in that period before she could write a single word. In contrast, a writer whose novels are set in the financial world told me how he does research: 'I write until I get to something I don't know, and then I look it up and keep writing.' He also has an expert read his manuscript when he's done the first draft to make sure he hasn't got anything wrong.

This man has written half a dozen novels. The other person has written none. But she's done a lot of research and by the time she dies, she'll be an expert.

If you are not moving forward with your project, ask these questions:

- What would you need in order to move forward just one step?
- Where can you get it easily and quickly?
- If you can't get it now, what other parts of the project can you work on?
- If you can't get it now and you can't work on any other parts of the project, what would happen if you moved forward anyway and came back and fixed the gaps later?

Yes, the conditions may not be ideal, you may have to blunder forward – but you'll still be moving in the right direction.

Look for the quirk

THE PRINCIPLE

In a bland world, the quirks stand out

How many products or services are interesting enough that you talk about them to friends? This is called word of mouth and it's the cheapest, most effective form of marketing there is. If you look for the quirks in your projects, you will find the key to word of mouth.

Let's face it, most products and services do the job but they are bland. I go shopping at Tesco or Sainsbury's, I buy office supplies at Ryman, I get coffees at Caffè Nero, but very seldom do I ever mention it to friends. Why? There's nothing out of the ordinary about any of these. In fact, I'm having a hard time coming up with any examples of extraordinary shopping experiences to cite in this book, but let's look at some quirks in other arenas:

- A product from Dave's Gourmet, called Lucky Nuts – every tenth nut is super hot. They've brought Russian roulette to snack foods.
- The ladies in the casinos in Las Vegas who bring you free drinks while you're playing the slot machines. Yes, I know – they are just designed to keep you there, losing money. And by the time you've tipped them, you've paid for the drink anyway – but it still seems like getting something free.
- The masseuses on certain Virgin Airlines flights who rub your weary shoulders as you wing in luxury across the ocean. Too bad Upper Class costs a fortune (I got it with Air Miles, and now I'm ruined for Economy travel for ever).
- At the gym, the personal trainer who gives you a free session on your birthday.

The characteristics of these appealing quirks and extras is that they are unexpected. By definition, the expected is the norm and not something we're likely to talk about. It's the pleasant surprise, the out of the ordinary that people remember.

I mentioned one more example previously, from the workshops I present. At some point in the afternoon, I hand out sealed envelopes and ask people not to open them until everybody has one. Then I have them open them in unison and take out the contents, and sniff it. What's in the envelope? A peppermint tea bag. The smell of peppermint refreshes you, which is a good thing when people are a bit lethargic after lunch.

That's a key point: the quirk should make sense, not just be something silly for the sake of being different. Seeing 30 or 40 people all sniffing tea bags always makes everybody laugh, which also helps enliven the session. It's a small thing but years later people still mention it with a chuckle.

As you go through the development process, occasionally think about what you can do that's quirky and adds to the value of the product or service. When you align the quirk with the personality you want your project to have, you have a winning combination.

Website bonus

At www.CreativityNowOnline.com, click on the 'Creativity Now!' button. Bonus 16 is a round-up of quirks that work.

Have a Plan B

THE PRINCIPLE

The Boy Scouts were right: it pays to be prepared

Some people say you should act as though failure is impossible. While that's admirable for its fighting spirit, I prefer the less zingy but more likely to succeed: 'Act as though failure is unlikely, but have a Plan B just in case.'

What this means in practice is identifying each key component of the project and having at least a rough idea of what you could do in case things don't go according to plan.

A British friend who is a public relations consultant based in Los Angeles learned this some years ago when she organised a Prince Andrew lookalike contest to coincide with his visit to that city. The contest was sponsored by a travel agency, and two local TV stations said they would send out camera crews to cover it. The day before the event I asked my friend how many people had signed up to participate in the contest. She said, 'Oh, I haven't asked for sign-ups, I assume they will just show up.' I posed the question of just how embarrassed she (and her client) would be if no contestants actually came. We quickly came up with Plan B – her accountant, her nephew, a friend of mine and I would attend and, if necessary, take part in the contest.

On the day, there were only two legitimate contestants, and one of those was an elderly homeless man who happened to be passing. The prize was awarded to the other legitimate contestant, who at least was roughly the right age and height, and the contest got coverage mainly for the fact that most of the contestants looked absolutely nothing like Prince Andrew. But the stories did mention the sponsoring travel agency, so the mission was accomplished.

To concoct a Plan B strategy follow these four steps:

1. List the key actions required by you or others to create your project. This will need updating fairly frequently.
2. For each of the key actions, jot down who could help if needed, and how you could rearrange your schedule if necessary.
3. For each of the actions someone else has to carry out, jot down a back-up person or business that could be called upon in an emergency. For instance, I keep handy the addresses of a couple of print shops in case my usual supplier is too overwhelmed with big jobs.
4. If you are relying on crucial equipment, have a list of places that could repair or replace it if it goes wrong. I rely heavily on my computer so I have information handy about a couple of places where I can hire a temporary replacement quickly if my Mac needs to be repaired.

With luck, your Plan A will work out most of the time, but having a Plan B means that what otherwise would be emergencies become merely inconveniences. Plus you sleep better at night.

Make a not-to-do list

THE PRINCIPLE

If what you're doing isn't moving you forward, then it's holding you back

Everybody is familiar with the to-do list. Sometimes it's equally important to have a not-to-do list of the things that discourage you or hold you back from putting in the time necessary to make your project a reality.

Here are some items to get you started:

- During working hours, do not watch television 'for just a little while'.
- Do not think about how much money J. K. Rowling or the superstar in your field is making with products that may be no better than yours.

- Do not review your rejection letters.
- Do not think about how many people in your field were successful before they reached the age you are now.
- During working hours, do not read your favourite newspaper or magazines 'for inspiration'.
- Do not alphabetise your books 'because it will make it easier to find things'.
- Do not start shaving any of your body parts because it's easier than working on your project.
- Do not answer any of those 'you have won the lottery' or 'a Nigerian banker will give you a million pounds for helping to transfer money that belonged to a person who died in a plane crash and has no living relatives' just in case one of them might actually be for real.

No doubt you have your own list of displacement activities. Go write that list and post it where you can see it. The problem with distractions is that they sneak up on you and suck you in, and it's only a couple of hours later that you snap out of your trance and realise you've wasted a big part of the day. By making them specific and visible, they are easier to conquer.

Embrace procrastination

THE PRINCIPLE

Working with, not against, procrastination can help you get things done

The usual response to procrastination is opposing it head-on, trying to use sheer willpower to do what we are resisting. As you may have noticed, it seldom works, or at least seldom for very long. Procrastination is a more sophisticated phenomenon than it may first appear. Here are some points to consider and the actions you can take to harness the power of procrastination:

1 If your procrastination doesn't have any negative consequences, you're doing a good job of assessing when to start the task, even if you could have started earlier. You are one of those rare people who really does work best under pressure. **Action:** Determine whether your habit of delaying work on a project has any negative consequences. If not, don't worry about it.

2 If you know you could have done better if you'd started earlier, try dipping into the task and doing a little bit as you go along. For some people, procrastination is about not wanting to finish a task, so you can put that off until the last minute, but when you reach that point you'll find you've done most of the work already. **Action:** Allocate small chunks of time to work on the project. (There's more on this in the section called 'Chunk and micro-chunk'.)

3 If you like the excitement of putting things off, find another way of getting that buzz. **Action:** Play 'to-do list roulette'. Write each task you want to achieve today on a separate index card. Turn them over and mix them up. Select one, turn it over and do that task. The element of chance may give you the adrenaline rush you crave.

4 BONUS IDEA: Here's a pre-procrastination tip. Your subconscious mind can be working on one thing while your conscious mind is working on something else. Creativity experts confirm that this germination or incubation period is important, but it only works if you plant the seed first. If you make yourself aware of what is required and then put it aside, your subconscious mind has something to work with. **Action:** Give your brain something to work with on the next-but-one project or next-but-one task you're planning. When the time comes to do it, you will find that you have a head start.

The key is not to see procrastination as an either/or thing: 'I do things perfectly according to other people's idea of a perfectly rational schedule' or 'I procrastinate.' Treat it as a process that can be managed to give you the best results based on your personality and preferences.

Website bonus

At www.CreativityNowOnline.com, click on the 'Creativity Now!' button. Bonus 17 is a link to an eight-part mini-course in overcoming procrastination.

Be the staff

THE PRINCIPLE

There's a hard-working staff ready to be employed – in your mind

If you're lucky enough to employ a development person, an engineering department, computer programmers, marketing and salespeople, public relations consultants, accountants and every other kind of staff required to turn your idea into reality, congratulations, you can jump ahead to the next section. For most of us, though, there is no staff or at least not enough to cover all the functions described.

That's why *you* have to be the staff. In other words, you have to be able to switch your viewpoint or perspective at will, to consider your project from all of these vantage points as you develop it. Even if you are not an expert, probably you have enough of an understanding of each function to give yourself valuable input as you go along.

The goal is to avoid, for example, a product that is beautiful and functional but can't possibly be produced at a price that makes it competitive with similar products already on the market. You may think nobody makes such a mistake, but a couple of the contestants on the *Dragons' Den* TV series were selling terrific ethnic food but didn't seem to realise, until the 'Dragons' pointed it out, that they were selling the product for less than it was costing them.

If the members of your imaginary staff are given the chance to have input at the major stages of the project, you will be able to anticipate problems and often to correct for them as you proceed.

Here are the core perspectives you need to consider:

- **The engineer's:** Is the product or service able to provide the desired function efficiently and effectively?
- **The designer's:** Does the product's or service's form or format support those functions and create an aesthetically agreeable experience?
- **The marketing person's:** Does the product or service have an appealing personality that will make it a strong brand?
- **The salesperson's:** Does it have a unique selling proposition (something that sets it apart from the competition)? Does it compare favourably with similar products or services?
- **The accountant's:** Can it be produced at a reasonable cost? Is there enough money to cover the development and marketing?

You don't need to have all the answers right from the start. Every innovation encounters obstacles relating to one or more of these factors, and sometimes you have to forge ahead and trust that you'll find solutions down the line. However, the sooner you alert yourself to possible problems, the more likely it is that you'll find solutions. That's a good reason to convene regular meetings of your staff – even if they're all sitting in your chair.

Chunk and micro-chunk

THE PRINCIPLE

When you find yourself avoiding tasks, breaking them up into chunks helps overcome your resistance

You may already have run across the strategy of 'chunking' tasks down into smaller components to overcome your resistance to doing them. Certainly something daunting like 'write a book' becomes more manageable when you convert it into tasks like 'outline chapter 1 with a mind map' and 'write the first three pages of chapter 1'.

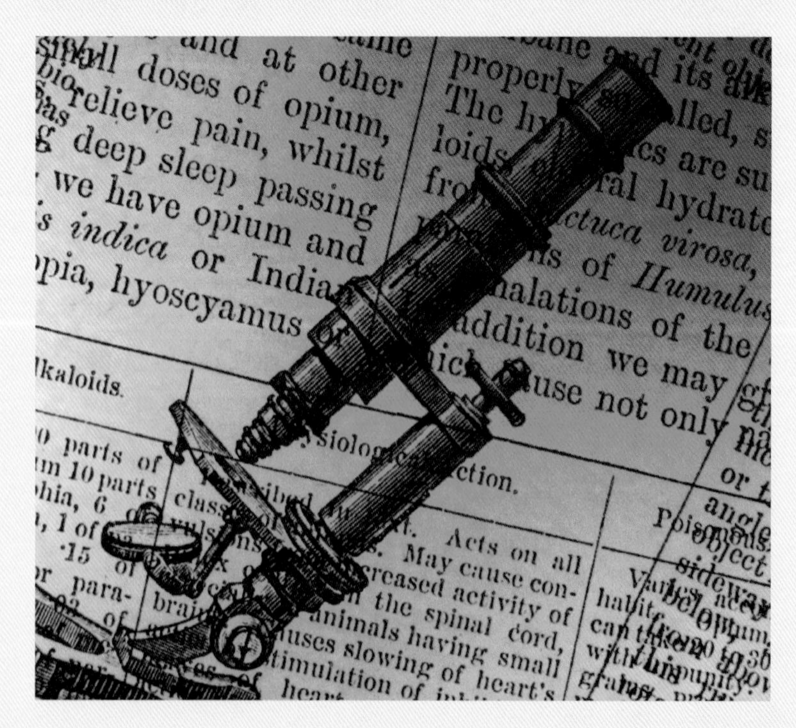

For some people even that is not enough, and for those I recommend what I call micro-chunking. That means breaking down the chunks even more, to the point where they may be so small as to seem ridiculous.

For instance, let's say you have been transferring the task of writing an invoice from one day to another (it's a mystery why so many of us, including me, resist writing invoices when it means we'll get paid). Invoicing someone is not a major task, but if you have put it off for several days, it's a candidate for micro-chunking. Here's how it might break down:

- **Day 1:** Make a note of the name and address of the person you'll be sending the invoice to.
- **Day 2:** On the same sheet of paper, write down the description of what service or product you supplied and the amount you will be billing.
- **Day 3:** Fill out the invoice.
- **Day 4:** Print it out.
- **Day 5:** Post it.

If that looks a bit ridiculous, that's the intention. In most cases once you've done the first chunk or certainly the first two chunks, you'll feel silly delaying another day and so you'll just complete the task. But knowing that you don't *have* to, that you can spend literally only a minute or two on each chunk, takes away the resistance.

When any task has been on your to-do list for more than three days, try chunking. If that doesn't do the trick, switch to micro-chunking.

Use timepods

THE PRINCIPLE

Focusing your activity for 45 minutes at a time increases your productivity

The biggest enemy of productivity is distractions. In an earlier section in this part, I mentioned MADs (Massive Action Days), a somewhat radical way to gain momentum on a project. It's not always practical to take MADs, so now I offer you a mini-version, timepods.

A timepod is a 45-minute period of time in which you focus all your attention on one task. The steps are as follows:

1. At the top of a sheet of paper, write down exactly what you intend to accomplish during the 45-minute period.
2. Make sure you have all necessary materials at hand. When the 45-minute period starts, you should not have to stop to look for files, or a stapler, or a pen.
3. Make sure you will not be interrupted for 45 minutes. That means switching on the answer-phone, not checking emails, not receiving visitors. In some cases this may mean going somewhere else for that 45 minutes – another office, a coffee shop, a nearby library.
4. Set a timer or a wristwatch alarm for 45 minutes.
5. Work with focus and concentration, avoiding any temptation to do anything other than the task at hand.
6. When the time is up, if you are not within 5 additional minutes of finishing what you described, stop. Take a 5-minute break. Walk around a little or do some simple exercises. Get a drink of water.
7. If your job requires it, take 10 minutes to catch up with phone messages or urgent emails.

8 Repeat the process. Gradually you will get better at judging how much you can achieve in the 45 minutes and at eliminating any obstacles or distractions that sneak in.

If you use even just four timepods during the course of an 8-hour day, you will find that your productivity more than doubles.

Use the Einstein levels

THE PRINCIPLE

One way to get over a block is to change the level at which you consider the problem

Albert Einstein said that you cannot solve a problem at the level at which is was created.

What follows is my own interpretation of the process, not Einstein's (as far as I'm aware he never went into detail on this). I begin by stating the basic task I'm finding problematic. Let's suppose that I am offering a workshop and have not been able to find enough people to sign up for it.

First we reduce the project to the basic steps we would usually follow:

1. Publicise the workshop.
2. Enrol paying customers.
3. Give the workshop.
4. Make money from the workshop.

If we try to solve the problem at the same level, we would just try to do one or more of these a bit better. That might mean sending out more press releases, reducing prices or adding some additional value by handing out more support materials. In each case we're trying for incremental improvement.

If we follow Einstein's advice, we will step up a level. Now we will be looking for a new way to reach the outcome, rather than optimising the current means to that end.

In our example, the end result is to generate revenue from the workshop. How else can I do that, without going through the first three steps? Ideas that come to mind include:

- Get sponsorship from a company so I only need to convince one person (the corporate officer) to spend money instead of the 50 or so who attend.
- Forget about doing it live. Do it on video and sell the DVDs.
- Give it for free and thereby attract enough people so that back-of-the-room sales of my books, CDs and DVDs generate the revenue.

We could step up another level, at which point the object is to come up with alternatives to the outcome itself. In that case, I would have to question whether giving workshops is the best way to make money.

Going up three levels becomes even more philosophical and questions whether the values represented by the outcome are valid. In this case, that would mean examining whether I'm doing the right thing by trying to earn money. By this level, we're pretty close to Zen-type thinking.

Most of the time, going up just one level is the most productive on a practical level. To sum up, here is that process:

1. Describe as basically as you can what you are trying to accomplish.
2. Instead of trying to improve the steps leading to the desired outcome, brainstorm new ways of achieving the outcome.
3. Evaluate these new solutions and if they seem more likely to work than what you were doing originally, implement them.

Give it a try. If it was good enough for Einstein…

Putting it all together

THE PRINCIPLE

Having a plan for the entire creative process improves your chance of success

It's time for you to go into action with your creative project or product. You've read all the techniques but sometimes it's still difficult to figure out how to put it all together. In this section I present a roadmap you can apply to any project.

I suggest that you get a new notebook or open a new document on your computer to record your answers and your ideas as you go through the process.

How long each step takes depends on how well formed the idea is already, how big a project it is, how much or little you will need the input and support of others, and so on. It's best not to rush it but also not to get hung up on any one step. If there are gaps that you know you'll be able to fill in later, move on and keep the momentum going.

I've illustrated each step with examples from one of my goals – creating an outstanding website to accompany this book. When you go to the site (www.CreativityNowOnline.com) you'll be able to judge for yourself whether or not I've achieved what I set out to do.

STEP ONE: Describe the dream

Start with a general description of what you want to create. No need to get specific at this point, and don't worry yet about limitations. Aim high! You can always scale back later if you need to, but start with a dream that fires your imagination.

My dream is to create a website that gives visitors the inspiration and tools to bring their creative projects into the world. I'd also like it to reflect my own creativity.

Now describe your dream for your project. If you're not sure yet of what it is, go back to Part 1 and use the methods you think would help you the most.

STEP TWO: Describe what elements would make the project as good as you hope it will be

Brainstorm what your project will require in order to fulfil its potential. Let's say you want to write a book that will enchant and delight both children and adults. That might require creating a gripping story that keeps readers eager to find out what happens next, and a protagonist with whom children can identify but whom adults find interesting as well.

You may already have some elements of your project in mind, but I'm asking you to step into the shoes of your target audience and use their desires and needs as a starting point.

In my example, for the inspirational aspect of the website I believe visitors will want some role models – people who have overcome obstacles to create something wonderful, whether large or small. They would also appreciate some encouragement during the difficult stages. And they might be happy if the site could somehow help them get recognition for their creative achievements.

Make a list of what your target audience probably wants from the kind of project you are creating. If you're not sure, find some targets and ask them. You can also use many of the tools in the 'Originating' part to help you.

STEP THREE: Get specific about the features of your project.

Having described in general terms what you hope to give your target audience, now it's time to get specific. Generate as many ideas as possible for how you could provide those features. You can use the brainstorming methods in the 'Originating' part to help you. Write down even the crazy ideas, save the judging for the next step.

Going back to the example of the novel, you might brainstorm the kinds of protagonists, whether animal, human or alien, that might enchant readers. You might also generate fascinating settings, such as Atlantis, strange other worlds in another universe, or just an ordinary household but seen in new ways. To involve the readers more it could be an ebook or a regular book related to an online game.

Some of my ideas for the website are: video interviews with highly creative people all over the world, revealing their process and advice; guided visualisations to put visitors in touch with their own strength and determination; a hotline they can call if they're discouraged, answered by the Dalai Lama, who will gently encourage them (I told you we're not censoring ourselves at this stage!); a part of the site where visitors can ask questions, share ideas and celebrate their achievements.

Generate as many ideas for your project as possible. I recommend doing this in short sessions spread out over several days or even several weeks. You may also want to get colleagues and friends involved – the more ideas the better.

STEP FOUR: Narrow down the options

In this phase we start to get more realistic and jettison the ideas that aren't going to work.

First to go in the winnowing should be any ideas that you now see wouldn't actually be relevant or useful.

Next consider which ideas seem impossible, but don't dismiss them until you have brainstormed whether you can come up with possible versions. For instance, while I concede that the Dalai Lama isn't going to be staffing my hotline, it gave me the idea of having a series of short recordings from his speeches or interviews that would be triggered when a site visitor clicks on the panic button.

If you're tempted to dismiss some things because they would be too expensive, think about whether there might be a way to do something similar more cheaply. I may not be able to travel the world doing interviews (especially as in my dream I was going first class all the way) but I should be able to record them via video phone calls.

As with the previous step, give yourself plenty of time. When you're done you'll have a solid list of ideas, but they probably won't have much shape yet.

STEP FIVE: Build your framework and your plan

Now it's time to see how you can put together your ideas to construct the foundation or skeleton of your project. Begin by considering which ideas might be combined or connected. This is where some of the methods in this 'Applying' part, such as making a mind map of the various parts of the project, will help.

In the case of my website, I can see that the ideas I generated fall into several categories: inspirational, educational and experiential (chances for visitors to share their creativity at the site). I also know I want the site to look creative so I want to go beyond the usual Wordpress template format.

Construct a plan of action with a rough timeline. You can use the action map format you saw earlier or a flow chart or any method you find useful. I do recommend having a printout handy rather than keeping everything only on your computer. Allow from 25 per cent to 50 per cent more time than you think it will take. Research has shown that most people underestimate by that margin and my own experience unfortunately confirms it.

I am allocating one month for the new website design, two months to generate the core content and one month for my web designer to implement the design and add the content. Even allowing slippage of 25 per cent, the site will be ready quite a while before the book is released, which is important. If we can get the publisher's sales reps to look at an impressive working site then that might increase their enthusiasm for the book when they talk to book shop managers.

If it's a complex project you can create an action map for each of its smaller chunks. For instance, if you plan to self-publish a book you can break the process down into writing, self-publishing and marketing. Each of these would have their own plans with many smaller steps.

You may not yet be sure how to accomplish some of the tasks. For those, repeat the steps you've already followed for the project as a whole. If you need to raise money to fund your self-publishing venture, for instance, you could start with the dream amount, then consider the more practical version, and brainstorm ways to get it (perhaps asking friends and family for an investment, crowdfunding or selling some of your things on eBay). Then you'd pick the best option and plan how and when to do it.

STEP SIX: Do it!

This is the implementation step. Too many creative people start the process here instead of taking the time to think and plan. Often their efforts are unfocused and chaotic. That makes implementation more difficult, they get discouraged and they abandon what could have been good projects.

Most creative people don't know about the implementation strategies and tools you've encountered in this 'Applying' part. Any time you are unsure of how to do something or find unexpected obstacles blocking your progress, check this part and you'll find a way forward.

It's useful to be aware that somewhere around the middle of implementing a project most people experience what Seth Godin calls 'the dip'. That is, a point at which you've devoted a lot of time and energy to your project but you're still a long way from the end and you feel depleted. This is when you may be tempted to give up. Usually that would be a mistake. If possible, take a short break and get back to work.

If your inner critic gets too loud, return to the 'Dreaming' part and review how to convert the critic to a constructive inner guide. It may be necessary to repeat that process several times as you implement your project.

For a large project don't forget to celebrate the milestones as well as the final result; that will also help take you through to completion.

STEP SEVEN: Evaluate and improve

You're done!

Actually....you're never done.

When you've sent your brainchild into the world you'll get feedback, both positive and negative. Hearing the latter can be painful but also useful. Eliminate any criticism that isn't constructive and use the rest either to improve the current project or apply the lessons to your next one.

When you've done all these, congratulate yourself. In the meantime, of course, you will have had several, or maybe several dozen, new ideas, so soon it'll be time to start the process all over again. That's why I end this section with one reminder to apply to all the steps: **enjoy the journey**.

adapting

pting

4

When you're trying to turn a great idea into a great product or service, it can feel like you're alone. But there are people doing this every day, and you can learn from their experience.

In this part you'll meet 25 people/companies that have been successful at realising their creative dreams. In each case you'll discover the creative principles and the methods they used. As well as being inspired, you can adapt their approach to make a success of your project.

I'd love to feature your creative triumph in a future edition of this book. Read on, benefit from these experiences and get to work.

Your future is waiting.

They became successful writers

THE PRINCIPLE

Working hard is just as important as working smart

The Atlanta Journal-Constitution ran an interview with Peter Bowerman, who is a commercial writer and author of *The Well-Fed Writer*. There was one sentence that really struck me as revealing the key element of success:

> ***'I began my writing career in January 1994 by making more than 1,000 phone calls to seek commercial writing jobs ... by May, I was paying all my bills.'***

This is where the rubber meets the road: Action!

- → A thousand phone calls
- → A hundred query letters
- → Fifty meetings

And a bunch of manuscripts, screenplays, articles or other projects where you learn what you're doing before one sells.

And let's not forget preparation. An even bigger success story is that of the late Stephen J. Cannell, the writer-producer noted for *The Rockford Files, The A-Team, Hunter, 21 Jump Street* and many more. At one point, his was the most successful TV production company in Hollywood.

In an interview in *Script* magazine, he revealed the secret of his early success when he was pitching ideas for television:

> ***'I would spend nine days getting ready for a 45-minute meeting ... you have to over-perform. It's the secret almost nobody's willing to do. A few people are, but most aren't. Most people look to the right and left and see how much effort is being put in, and they match it. But I was willing to do it ... [and that's] why I got where I wanted to go.'***

I had the pleasure of interviewing Cannell a couple of times and he was always generous with his time and advice. After selling his TV production company he forged another successful career as a novelist, working just as hard at that as he had at writing and producing TV series.

We creative people get very excited about inspiration. These two success stories remind us that perspiration is also important.

His little lessons changed his life – and many others', too

THE PRINCIPLE

It doesn't take high-tech or a big team to change the world

In 2006 Sal Kahn worked in finance, so he was the logical person for his young cousins to turn to when they had problems learning science and maths. He started making YouTube videos to tutor them remotely.

His relatives weren't the only ones who found his lessons useful. Six years later, he's posted more than 2600 micro-lessons and his work has come to be known as the Khan Academy. It's now his full-time job and the videos have been seen more than 67 million times.

The tutorials, which cover mathematics, finance, history, physics, chemistry, biology, astronomy, computer science and economics, are free, supported by donations and underwriting from foundations. In 2010 Google announced a grant of $2 million to support the creation of more courses and to translate the Academy's content into more languages.

By the way, Khan's face never appears in the videos, they're all done with illustrations, diagrams and screen captures.

From a few mini-lessons for his relatives, Khan has gone to the goal of creating 'the world's first free, world-class virtual school where anyone can learn anything'.

They got money from the crowd

THE PRINCIPLE

You can get customers to finance a product before you make it

David Lasky and Frank Young are artist/writers whose dream is to create a 192-page full-colour graphic novel that tells the story of country music's first family, the Carter Family. They proposed it to a publisher and got an advance, but not enough to pay the bills for the long time it would take to write, draw and colour this epic work.

They decided to try to see whether they could raise $5000 using a crowdfunding site called Kickstarter.

At Kickstarter.com people who want to raise money to produce a book, a song collection, a board game, a sculpture, or pretty much anything else creative, present their idea and ask members of the public to pledge some money towards it. They offer rewards geared to the level of the pledge. A campaign can raise more than its target amount, but if it fails to reach the target the people who did pledge are not charged.

One project offered a name or word of your choice written in calligraphy for $5, and more words for higher levels of donation. In exchange, the artist would get to practise her craft and buy materials. Her initial goal was $500, but she ended up raising more than $3600.

And Lasky and Young? They raised more than $8000, so it's back to the drawing board – in a good way.

Her gift made her rich

THE PRINCIPLE

If you create something you care about, others will care too

In 2000, Jacquie Lawson, an English artist living in the village of Lurgashall, West Sussex, created an animated Christmas card featuring her dog, Chudleigh, her cats and her fifteenth-century cottage. She emailed it to a few friends and then went on holiday for three weeks.

When she returned she had 1600 emails in her inbox. Her friends had passed the card on to other friends, who also passed it on, and so on. Her email address was on it and now all these people wanted to know whether she had other cards.

She decided to turn it into a business offering animated cards for many occasions. At the moment she has 126 designs, which can be accessed by paying a membership fee of £6.25 per year (her site is **www.jacquielawson.com**).

Lawson has more than 250,000 subscribers. Have you done the maths yet? That's more than £1.5 million a year! Despite what her website describes as 'the enormous cost of servers and such-like', and the fact that she now has a nephew and niece and a neighbour working for her, that's a huge profit margin.

The best part of the story, for me, is that it all started with something she did for the love of it. When your creative instincts come from a desire to create something that gives joy to others, your chances of commercial success also increase.

The real experts led them to success

THE PRINCIPLE

The people who use what you make are the people to listen to

Chris Miller is the founder and Chief Creative Officer of Earth Products, a highly successful action sports clothing and accessories company. He is a former professional skateboarder, so he's in direct touch with what the market wants. But he says his biggest business secret is that he also relies on current professional athletes to give him input on product design and the marketing of his brands.

That doesn't sound like such a breakthrough idea – after all, almost every sports-related business has some high-profile athlete as a spokesperson. But Miller says that his company doesn't get just endorsements, they get specific feedback and ideas for improving the products. Furthermore, they ask not only pros but also top-level regional and local athletes, who are very influential on the entire market.

Why do so few businesses really pay attention to this kind of feedback? Possibly because by the time the feedback comes in, the product is so far into development that making changes would be very expensive.

You can avoid falling into that trap by consulting your potential customers or clients at all the stages of your development. You can use surveys, questionnaires, discussion groups and online forums as a way to harvest input that will make the difference between failure and success.

Word of mouth took it from free to famous

THE PRINCIPLE

Offering your product free can lead to fame and fortune

Simon Tofield didn't set out to produce an internet phenomenon, it just turned out that way. He created some simple, funny, black-and-white animations about his cat, called, fittingly enough, 'Simon's Cat'. He posted them on YouTube and they became an immediate hit, with more than 20 million hits. They also won awards including Best Comedy at the British Animation Awards and YouTube's Blockbuster Award.

Now publisher Cannongate has won a spirited auction for the world rights to two illustrated books by Tofield and they are in discussion with a number of film, television and merchandising companies about taking advantage of the Simon's Cat brand.

The key to what may turn out to be a hugely profitable franchise was, first, a charming product with wide appeal (there is no dialogue, so the cartoons can be appreciated worldwide) and, second, exposing it for free to people who could then let all their friends know about it.

Giving things away goes counter to the old model of marketing, but via the internet it can offer you a quick way to establish yourself and create conditions for profiting massively later.

A change of location made dinner profitable

THE PRINCIPLE

Sometimes changing where you offer your product changes everything

How would you like to host a dinner party 130 feet up in the air? No, not on a low-flying aeroplane but around a table hoisted by a giant crane. Sounds bizarre, but it's the premise of a successful business called 'Dinner in the Sky'.

The brainchild of David Ghysells, a Belgian marketing executive, it allows 22 diners to be strapped into their chairs while being served by waiters and waitresses standing in an aisle in the centre of the table. You can even ask to have an opera singer up there with you to entertain your guests. Or you can hire a second crane to lift a platform holding a band so you can have music while you eat.

The costs vary according to the menu and how long you are in the air, but in Belgium a leisurely session for 22 people runs to around £10,000, while shorter sessions in Las Vegas come with a much lower price tag, at around £4000.

The company has partners in 30 countries and has lifted more than 125,000 people. Clients include corporations wanting to impress customers and well-heeled individuals wanting to host a dinner party unlike any other. The company isn't stopping at dinners: you can also ask for 'Marriage in the Sky', 'Lounge in the Sky' and 'Showbiz in the Sky.'

As crazy as it sounds, the basic concept simply is a (radical) change of location for an otherwise mundane activity. Sometimes that's all it takes to create something amazing.

They're winning breakthrough ideas

THE PRINCIPLE

One way to get great ideas is to create a contest

In 1996 the California-based X Prize Foundation offered a $10 million prize for the first successful private space flight. It was won by SpaceShipOne. In 2008 they added further prizes of up to $30 million for solutions to problems relating to energy, the environment and education, among others.

The Foundation's chairman and CEO, Peter H. Diamandis, told the *Harvard Business Review* that with a contest the entrants are not only after the money, they also enjoy the thrill of the chase, the potential fame and the benefits to humanity. And companies or rich individuals who sponsor a prize get to put their money to good use.

The Foundation is after big breakthroughs and considering big prizes for things like a programme that can boost a child's reading level by two years in the space of six months. For most of the prizes anybody can enter, which ensures that even people who have 'crazy' ideas can get them considered.

Of course, not many people or organisations can afford those kinds of prizes, so the Foundation is exploring a way to create smaller rewards, of between $10,000 and $1 million, to tackle local problems.

You can take this even lower in terms of the level of financial reward. You might be surprised by how little it takes (financially) to get people coming up with ideas to help you solve your challenges, as long as there is some recognition for the winners. It could be a great way to harness the power of some fellow creative thinkers and offer a win–win outcome for everyone.

He combined two trends and created a third

THE PRINCIPLE

You can create a new business by combining trends

Trend 1: Food enriched with vitamins and minerals

Trend 2: People willing to spend more money on their pets

Marco Giannini spotted these trends and figured out a way to combine them. His product is Dogswell, dog treats infused with nutrients to help pets stay healthy. In 2004 he invested $30,000 (about £20,000) of his own money to produce the first lorry-load of sample treats and took them around to 200 independent pet stores in California.

The orders came rolling in and he grossed about £338,000 in sales his first year. Four years later he had sales of £10.8 million. That's a lot of treats. Next: Catswell.

Michael Sands, co-founder of Lesser-Evil Brand Snack Company, did something similar, this time reconciling two directly opposed trends.

Trend 1: People love to eat snack foods

Trend 2: People want to cut back on junk foods

His solution was to provide snacks with all the sinful flavours of junk food, but without so many of the preservatives and high-calorie ingredients. The company's motto is 'Stop bad snacking!' It addressed both trends, and as a result reached annual sales of more than $1.4 million (about £1 million) in only three years.

Most people who pay attention to trends try to take advantage of only one, and therefore face a lot of competition. If you can find a way to combine two, as Giannini and Sands did, you are more likely to come up with a product or service that is unique.

They found customers who weren't being served

THE PRINCIPLE

Look for customers who are not being served – and serve them

Will Ramsay liked art but found the atmosphere at most galleries unwelcoming and intimidating. Certain that many others must feel the same way, he started the Affordable Art Fair in Battersea Park in 1999. The first one attracted 10,000 visitors who could stroll around looking at paintings in a friendly, informal atmosphere, with prices clearly indicated and not a whiff of snobbery.

Now Affordable Art Fairs take place biannually in London at two locations and annually in Bristol, Amsterdam, Paris and New York, with affiliate fairs in Sydney and Melbourne. Artwork prices range from £50 to £2500 with more than 150 artists taking part in each fair.

Another example is the company Holidaytaxis.com, started by Paul Stanyer. After working as a holiday rep in the Mediterranean for years, he realised that for many holidaymakers, spending their first hours at their destination on a transfer bus that stops at a series of hotels was not a great start to a holiday. At the same time, many tourists are suspicious of the local taxis, afraid they will be taken for a ride in more ways than one. His solution was to start a company that allows tourists to pre-order a taxi that will be waiting for them, with the fare clearly specified.

The company was such a hit that it now operates in 30 countries.

There is no shortage of unfilled needs – only a shortage of people creative enough to spot them and figure out how to fill them.

He deals with dirt – and cleans up

THE PRINCIPLE

Sometimes doing the opposite provides a new solution

Everybody is familiar with graffiti. Some people consider it art, many consider it vandalism: dirty (sometimes literally as well as metaphorically) messages that pollute the environment.

Artist Paul Curtis turned this around 180 degrees. Going by his graffiti name of Moose, Curtis creates his messages by cleaning urban surfaces and letting the cleaned part be the image. His work appears in Leeds and in Shoreditch, London, and his company, Symbollix, has been hired for ad campaigns by Microsoft, Iageo and others.

He uses stencils, brushes and water as well as sandpaper and razor blades to create images and words from sooty and grotty surfaces including pavements and tunnels.

At one point Leeds City Council threatened legal action against him, but you can't actually arrest people for cleaning a surface. Since then he's done work for the Metropolitan Police and both Scottish and English governments and has expanded his work to New York.

The creative person takes a contrarian position and finds ways to make it work. Thinking about the opposite of what most people are doing is a great starting point for a breakthrough.

They keep your memory alive after you're not

THE PRINCIPLE

Pushing boundaries opens up new possibilities

Facebook, Twitter and all manner of other social networking sites let you communicate easily with friends and family. Most of us would expect that communication to stop when we leave this life. But the people behind a company called I-Postmortem decided not to stop at the usual boundaries.

With their i-memorial service you can build your own virtual memorial and leave messages to be delivered after you're no longer around. You can upload video, audio, photos, text, music and documents to tell your own life story and perhaps say things you didn't want to say while you were alive.

The company has secure servers based in Switzerland. When they get proof of death, they make the person's account go live (so to speak) on the internet, as an i-tomb. Friends and family members can add tributes, and a post-mortem administrator, who may have been chosen by the departed, can control what's added.

It's too early to judge how successful the company will be but they get full marks for not letting conventional limits restrict their thinking. What boundaries could you push to create a whole new category for your product or service?

This time it's personal

THE PRINCIPLE

What feels tailor-made is profitable

Here's how Joanna Wivell described her business to me:

> ***'Having lived in Madrid for six years, I decided it was time to make the most of the fact that I am an English person and Spanish aficionado living in Spain. So the idea was to set up something which bridges the two cultures.'***

Her company is called Insider's Madrid (**www.insidersmadrid.com**) and she organises trips and events for large and small groups of English speakers visiting Spain. She says, 'Although I guide people through flamenco dancing, bullfighting, and tapas tours myself, I have been busy making contact with people who specialise in different areas to help me do it.'

The venues the company uses, as well as the guides, reflect a variety of interests. For instance, she says, 'I have just met an aristocrat who used to accommodate The Rolling Stones in his country house when they used to play in the North of Spain. We are planning on cocktail parties in his house in Madrid.' Another option is a Real Madrid night at the Bernabeu Stadium with pre-match cocktails.

If you're a fan of rock music, flamenco dancing, football or one of the other specialities on their books, doesn't that sound more interesting than the typical tour?

The key is to make the customers feel like the service was designed just for them. Not only will they be willing to pay a premium, it's something they'll talk about to all their friends when they get home – and that's priceless word-of-mouth advertising.

Metro
Sol

He's playing by the (biggest) book

THE PRINCIPLE

There's always interest in what is the most (anything)

The books published by Kraken Sports and Media are extreme. How extreme? Well, they weigh upwards of 40 kgs, measure nearly 2 feet square and are 850 pages long. And, oh yes, they cost between £1400 (their cheapest title) and £70,000.

The publisher, Karl Fowler, doesn't call it a book, he calls it an Opus. One example is *History of the Saatchi Gallery*, featuring more than 1000 images as well as essays by eminent art critics and collectors, and protected in an inlaid wooden case. It's an exclusive limited edition of 950, each individually numbered and signed by Charles Saatchi. The price was £2250, but all the copies were snapped up. As of this writing, you can still order their F1 Opus, *Champions Edition*, for £20,000. If you don't have that much in your wallet, not to worry, they have easy payment plans.

'We're doing something that's never been done before,' Fowler told *The Times*. 'It's something iconic.' That's not an overstatement: *The Times* reported that the Opus on Manchester United changed hands for £1 million.

These prices may sound like madness if you think of these as books, but in fact they are works of art containing many one-of-a-kind images. Fowler has said they fit in a niche that is resilient to almost any economic downturn. This makes sense when you hear that the million-pound Man U volume was number 777, bought by a collection of investors in the Middle East, where that is a lucky number.

The message is that there is always a lot of potential at the margins – certain people are willing to pay a lot to have the biggest and the best, or just something few other people have.

However, Opus aren't ignoring those of us with thinner wallets. They're making many of their titles available for the Kindle and the iPad. As of this writing, the Official Ferrari Opus HD for iPad, for instance, is available for about £5.

They made travel less taxing

THE PRINCIPLE

Adding unusual value to a routine service makes it stand out

About sixteen years ago Kevin and Belma Marshall bought an 1812 Colonial house near the charming historical town of Granby, Connecticut, and turned it into a bed and breakfast. So far, so ordinary. What made the venture a roaring success was creating a 'Tax & Relax' package.

Kevin is an accountant and people who bought the package got one night at the B&B, breakfast for two … and if they were US citizens he prepared their taxes. When they left, he completed the forms and sent off the tax returns within ten days.

Adding this kind of value took the business out of the ordinary. The Associated Press wire service did a story on the couple and their unique service. That led to further media coverage from CNN, USAToday.com, NYTimes.com, the *Wall Street Journal* and half a dozen others. The result was a flood of customers.

Currently the Inn is run by Bill and Nancy Ross, who don't offer the tax package but have added innovative special weekend events that continue to set the venue apart from most B&Bs.

Most bed-and-breakfast establishments might think of having flat-screen televisions or an extensive breakfast menu in order to stand out, but those are only incremental improvements. What really gets people's attention is adding something unexpected and unusual. What can you add to your endeavour?

They got people hooked

THE PRINCIPLE

Expose people to your products any way you can – if they like it they'll pay for more

In 1999 Moby's album *Play* was not selling well. He licensed all of the album's 18 tracks for use in commercials, television shows or films – the first time this had been done. People were exposed to the music, liked it, wanted to hear more and ended up buying more than 10 million copies of the album around the world.

Wayne Gould didn't invent Sudoku, but he did make it popular. Intrigued by a Sudoku book he saw in Tokyo, he wrote a computer program that generated Sudoku puzzles and rated their difficulty. His Pappocom Sudoku puzzles were picked up by more than 400 newspapers internationally. But instead of charging the papers for it, he made it free – as long as the publications promoted his books and computer program. The people who enjoyed doing the puzzles wanted more. Gould sold over 4 million books.

In both these examples the method of distribution became the key to the success of the products. Especially if the traditional ways of distributing your product or service are overcrowded or expensive, consider how you get them to your customers. As shown by Moby and Gould, once you get them hooked, they'll want more.

VOLUME

She changed the medium and they got the message

THE PRINCIPLE

Providing a product or service in a new medium makes it new

Juliet Huck's company, The Huck Group, is a Los Angeles graphic design firm with a unique mission: to make complicated courtroom testimony easy to understand. To this end they use magnetic boards, slides, illustrations, sound files – anything and everything that can present information in a clear and persuasive way.

As explained on their website (**www.thehuckgroup.com**), their process consists of making the complex simple, identifying key factors or 'decision points' in the story, and bringing the story to life by building layers of visual clues. It's all based on the premise that people comprehend and retain visual information more effectively than verbal information.

The company practises visually persuasive story-telling in marketing their own business, too, using a storybook to explain what the company does and to show samples of their previous work. It has led to work on many high-profile cases and a turnover in excess of $1 million a year.

The heart of any marketing and sales effort, whether the audience is a jury, a funding entity or a single customer, is story-telling. What story do you want to tell and how can you tell it most effectively?

She went back to the future

THE PRINCIPLE

'Lost' products or services can be rediscovered for profit

Once upon a time, etiquette was considered very important and children were expected to know how to behave in a variety of situations. In 2000, American Corrine Gregory thought it was time to revive that idea and founded the company The Polite Child. The company offers a programme called SocialSmarts, dedicated to 'developing excellent social skills in children of all ages – from toddlers to teens'.

The programme is offered via public and private schools, as private classes and by authorised providers across the country. The claimed benefits are giving young people strong self-esteem and confidence and the ability to handle a myriad of social interactions and situations.

With an increasing problem with bullying, violence in schools and children seemingly out of control, the company may find even greater demand for its services.

In your arena, what has been lost or gone out of fashion? Might it be time for a profitable comeback?

She went from 'vs' to 'and'

THE PRINCIPLE

Cooperating with competitors can create win–win situations

Valerie Young is the founder of Changing Course (**www.changingcourse.com**), where she sells a 'Dream Accelerator Kit' to help people find their true calling. When she decided to create a CD about how aspiring entrepreneurs could achieve their dreams, instead of trying to beat the competition, she courted two highly successful competitors, Barbara Sher (author of *I Could Do Anything If I Only Knew What It Was*) and Barbara Winter (author of *Making a Living without a Job*). They accepted her proposal that the three of them work together to produce and share the profits of a CD programme called *Making Dreams Happen*.

In a letter to *Entrepreneur* magazine, Young notes that women seem to be more open to this kind of cooperation, referring to the belief among many women that 'there is something wrong with a definition of success that says, "in order for me to win, someone else has to lose"'.

Who are your competitors? How could you cooperate in a venture that would be advantageous for all of you?

He unlocked his creativity

THE PRINCIPLE

Sometimes simplifying is the key to unlocking riches

Have you ever used a combination lock and forgotten the numbers? It has happened to most of us, and that's what gave inventor Todd Basche the idea for his 'Wordlock'. As the name suggests, it's a combination lock that uses letters instead of numbers. Instead of the numbers 54710, for instance, the lock could spell 'beach' – which would you find easier to remember?

It's an invention that made Basche the winner of the Staples 2004 Invention Quest Contest. The prize was $25,000 plus the agreement to sell the Wordlock at all Staples stores and on their website. Since then the line has expanded to include luggage locks, bicycle locks, padlocks and cable locks for computers.

Like many breakthroughs, this is one of those 'why didn't anybody think of this before?' ideas. As the website (**www.wordlock.com**) points out, it 'creates an amazing innovation to a category that hasn't seen a significant change since the 1800s'.

What product or service in your arena could be made simpler or easier to use?

He took a risk for Sin

THE PRINCIPLE

Showing (instead of just telling) can win converts

Frank Miller, author of the *Sin City* series of graphic novels, told his friends it wouldn't be possible to make a live-action film version of these books. He resisted all offers from Hollywood until young director Robert Rodriguez approached him with a unique proposal: come and watch him shoot a scene from one of the books for a day. If he liked what he saw, they would make a deal to give Rodriguez the right to make a film of *Sin City*. If not, Rodriguez would give him the short film from that day as a souvenir and that would be the end of the discussion.

Miller took him up on it. He went to Austin, Texas, and watched actors including Josh Hartnett play a scene from one of the short stories from the *Sin City* books in front of a green screen. On the same day, Rodriguez edited the footage and added music and special effects to complete the 3-minute film.

Miller was convinced. Rodriguez and Miller became co-directors of the film, which came out in 2005, grossing more than £100 million worldwide and spawning plans for a sequel.

They took a half-measure to promote safety

THE PRINCIPLE

To capture people's attention, show them something different

A sign on a construction site in Newcastle warns digger drivers, '9 ½ MPH SPEED LIMIT IN FORCE.'

Why nine and half? Why not ten?

Richard Hancock, project manager for the company Galliford Try, explains:

> *'If you put a 10 mph limit sign up, people barely notice it and go their own speeds. If you put nine-and-a-half miles an hour, then people do a double-take and stick to it.'*

It worked on the first site at which they tried it so now they're using it at others as well.

It's a good demonstration that what you use to get attention doesn't have to be expensive or complicated. Just different.

THEY TOOK A HALF-MEASURE TO PROMOTE SAFETY

She went from Mum to money

THE PRINCIPLE

Establishing an apparent one-to-one relationship wins you followers

Marla Cilley, also known as Fly Lady, nags people for a living. Every day she sends emails to her more than 400,000 followers, reminding them to get up, clean the sink, eat healthy food and take care of their skin. On average, her customers, mainly middle-aged American homemakers, receive 15 such messages a day. She also sells them branded T-shirts, bags, kitchen timers, dusters, books, calendars and more at her **www.flylady.net** website.

She receives about 5000 emails a day. One of them said, 'You are the mother I never had.' It's that personal connection that makes her customers feel like she's talking directly to them, guiding them with tips and encouragement, and making their days at home less lonely. Whenever she gets a testimonial for one of her new products, she copies it to the entire mailing list, which sparks a flood of new orders.

To keep in touch with her fans, Cilley does personal appearances at 'Flyfests', writes a self-syndicated column that appears every week in more than 200 newspapers and participates in a call-in satellite radio programme on worldtalkradio.net, where hers is the number one show. She's also written three popular books.

Being a surrogate mum pays well. Cilley's sales now exceed £3 million. She employs 24 people, including 6 just to deal with all the email.

Does Cilley really have a one-to-one relationship with more than 400,000 people? Of course not. However, by creating that illusion, she provides a valued service. Is there a way you could do the same?

She made the numbers add up

THE PRINCIPLE

Where there's frustration there's opportunity

Many creative people dislike keeping track of financial details. As a young entrepreneur, Jesicca Mah was no different but she decided to do something about it. Finding existing software like Excel or Quickbooks too complicated and time-consuming to learn, she and co-founder Andy Su decided to create an alternative.

Taking inspiration from Mint.com, a personal finance site, they and their team developed inDinero (**www.indinero.com**). It helps business owners monitor the financial health of their companies, and it claims you can learn how to use it in minutes rather than hours.

Its features include reminders of bills to pay and warnings if your account balances get low. The operation is expanding rapidly and adding features. Mah says their users are the greatest source of ideas for new features, which include mobile applications, ways to make tax filing easier and increasing the number of compatible international banking institutions.

Mah's advice is that when you have an idea, rather than trying to raise money, focus exclusively on your product and how it can benefit your target audience.

It's a great example of letting a personal frustration inspire a successful product.

EDERLANDSCHE BANK
100
GULD

She puts others first

THE PRINCIPLE

Skills that fill the pocketbook can also fill the heart

Twenty-five-year-old Tammy Tibbetts became a digital media expert in the course of her work as a journalist for several women's magazines. She began to wonder whether social media could be used to drive social change, specifically to help girls around the world to become the first in their family to graduate.

She and college student Christen Brandt started 'She's the First' as a media campaign to get groups of friends to sponsor a girl. They provided suggestions for enjoyable ways for the groups to raise funds and linked donors with sponsorship programmes for girls.

The girls are not the only ones to benefit: the programme also intends to foster leadership and self-awareness in young donors. The hope is to shape a rising generation of well-educated global leaders, future philanthropists and cross-cultural communicators.

The website (**www.shesthefirst.org**) features a map showing where fundraising events are taking place, facts relating to girls' education in the developing world, a blog and fundraising tips. In sheer numbers, the campaign is still small – it has led to sponsorship of about 80 girls so far – but the impact on those individuals is huge.

Tibbetts and her team are an excellent example of combining your expertise with something for which you have a passion to create a powerful force for good.

afterword

THE PRINCIPLE

You are creative and the world is waiting for your contribution

I hope this book has given you many new ways to dream, to be inspired by what others have done, to come up with breakthrough ideas and to turn them into reality. It may be a lonely quest at times and there will be setbacks and rejection, but you owe it to yourself and the world to create what only you can create.

Please have a look at all the extras behind the 'Creativity Now!' button on my website, **www.CreativityNowOnline.com**. That's also where you can contact me if you have any questions or – even better – to tell me about your success in creating something new and exciting. I believe you can do it and I wish you every success.

JURGEN WOLFF

about the author

JURGEN WOLFF is a writer whose books include: *Focus: Use the Power of Targeted Thinking, Marketing for Entrepreneurs, Your Writing Coach* and *Do Something Different.* He is a Neuro-Linguistic Programming practitioner and a certified hypnotherapist, and teaches creativity and writing courses internationally. He has also written more than 100 episodes for television series, including *Relic Hunter* and his original kids' series, *Norman Normal,* as well as TV movies, mini-series, films and plays produced in London, New York and Los Angeles. His website is **www.jurgenwolff.com**.

acknowledgements

PICTURE CREDITS

The publisher would like to thank the following for their kind permission to reproduce their photographs:

Pearson Education Ltd p.62; BananaStock p.200; BananaStock, Imagestate p.50; Brand X Pictures, Philip Coblentz p.118; Comstock Images p.211; construction photography.com, BuildPix p.98; Corbis p.125; Dan Dalton, Photodisc, Getty Images p.215; Digital Stock pp.29, 167; Digital Vision p.87; Digital Vision, Steve Rawlings p.47; Frederic Cirou, PhotoAlto Agency RF Collections, Getty Images p.170; Gai Coleman p.183; Harnett, Hanzon, Photodisc p.152; Imagestate, John Foxx Collection pp.1, 7, 10, 11, 12, 17, 19, 26, 40, 42, 59, 61, 65, 67, 70, 73, 88, 97, 115, 121, 135, 146, 149, 150, 155, 160, 179, 193, 197, 205, 207, 213, 216; M. Freeman, Photolink, Photodisc p.79; National Archives and Records Administration p.188; Pearson Education Asia Ltd, Coleman Yuen p.123; Pearson Education Ltd, Ann Cromack, Ikat Design p.51; Pearson Education Ltd, Jon Barlow p.45; Pearson Education Ltd, Jules Selmes pp.57, 191, 209, Pearson Education Ltd, MindStudio 9, Pearson Education Ltd, Studio 8 p.129; Peter Evans p.25; Photodisc pp.15, 83, 93, 94, 127, 132, 140, 143, 157, 176, 180, 187; Photodisc, C Squared Studios p.84; Photodisc, Cole Publishing Group, Victor Budnik p.116; Photodisc, Doug Menuez p.101; Photodisc, Karl Weatherly p.175; Photodisc, Nick Koudis p.144; Photodisc, Photolink pp.23, 32, 37, 91, 105, 107, 172, 203; Photodisc, Photolink, F. Schussler p.110; Photodisc, Steve Cole pp.68, 76, 185; Photodisc, StockTrek pp.21, 136; Photodisc, Tim Hall p.30; Steve Cole, Photodisc p.169; SuperStock, Ingram Publishing, Alamy pp.131, 195; The Illustrated London News Picture Library, Ingram Publishing, Alamy pp.35, 52, 80, 198; TongRo Image Stock, Alamy pp.39, 139.

Cover images: *Front*: Shutterstock.com: dgbomb

Every effort has been made to trace the copyright holders and we apologise in advance for any unintentional omissions. We would be pleased to insert the appropriate acknowledgement in any subsequent edition of this publication.

index